TEXT AND PER

General Editor: Michael Scott

The series is designed to introduce sixth-form and undergradu-
ate students to the themes, continuing vitality and performance
of major dramatic works. The attention given to production
aspects is an element of special importance, responding to the
invigoration given to literary study by the work of leading
contemporary critics.

The prime aim is to present each play as a vital experience in
the mind of the reader – achieved by analysis of the text in
relation to its themes and theatricality. Emphasis is accordingly placed on the relevance of the work to the modern reader
and the world of today. At the same time, traditional views are
presented and appraised, forming the basis from which a
creative response to the text can develop.

In each volume, Part One: *Text* discusses certain key themes
or problems, the reader being encouraged to gain a stronger
perception both of the inherent character of the work and also
of variations in interpreting it. Part Two: *Performance* examines
the ways in which these themes or problems have been handled
in modern productions, and the approaches and techniques
employed to enhance the play's accessibility to modern
audiences.

A Synopsis of the play is given and an outline of its major
sources, and a concluding Reading List offers guidance to the
student's independent study of the work.

HENRY THE FOURTH
Parts 1 and 2

Text and Performance

T. F. WHARTON

© T. F. Wharton 1983

All rights reserved. No part of this publication may be
reproduced or transmitted, in any form or by any means,
without permission.

First published 1983 by
THE MACMILLAN PRESS LTD
Companies and representatives
throughout the world

ISBN 0 333 33999 1 (pbk)

Typeset by
WESSEX TYPESETTERS LTD,
Frome, Somerset
Printed in Hong Kong

DISCARDED
WIDENER UNIVERSITY

WIDENER UNIVERSITY
WOLFGRAM
LIBRARY
CHESTER, PA.

PR
2809
.W55
1983

The paperback edition of this book is sold subject to the
condition that it shall not, by way of trade or otherwise,
be lent, resold, hired out, or otherwise circulated without
the publisher's prior consent, in any form of binding or cover
other than that in which it is published and without a similar
condition including this condition being imposed on the
subsequent purchaser.

CONTENTS

Illustrations will be found in Part Two.

ACKNOWLEDGEMENTS

Quotations of the text of the play are from the New Penguin Shakespeare edition (1968), edited by P. H. Davison.

The author wishes to thank the director and staff of the Nuffield Library at the Shakespeare Centre, Stratford-upon-Avon, for their courtesy and helpfulness; and the National Sound Archive, London, for the use of its resources.

TO MY SON
TOM

GENERAL EDITOR'S PREFACE

For many years a mutual suspicion existed between the theatre director and the literary critic of drama. Although in the first half of the century there were important exceptions, such was the rule. A radical change of attitude, however, has taken place over the last thirty years. Critics and directors now increasingly recognise the significance of each other's work and acknowledge their growing awareness of interdependence. Both interpret the same text, but do so according to their different situations and functions. Without the director, the designer and the actor, a play's existence is only partial. They revitalise the text with action, enabling the drama to live fully at each performance. The academic critic investigates the script to elucidate its textual problems, understand its conventions and discover how it operates. He may also propose his view of the work, expounding what he considers to be its significance.

Dramatic texts belong therefore to theatre and to literature. The aim of the 'Text and Performance' series is to achieve a fuller recognition of how both enhance our enjoyment of the play. Each volume follows the same basic pattern. Part One provides a critical introduction to the play under discussion, using the techniques and criteria of the literary critic in examining the manner in which the work operates through language, imagery and action. Part Two takes the enquiry further into the play's theatricality by focusing on selected productions of recent times so as to illustrate points of contrast and comparison in the interpretation of different directors and actors, and to demonstrate how the drama has worked on the modern stage. In this way the series seeks to provide a lively and informative introduction to major plays in their text and performance.

MICHAEL SCOTT

PLOT SYNOPSIS AND SOURCES

Part 1: Henry IV (Bolingbroke), having deposed the bad but rightful king, Richard II and caused his murder, seeks to atone by a crusade to the Holy Land. Domestic problems, however, intervene. A quarrel develops between the king and the Percy family, the northern lords who were formerly his allies. Henry's own sin of rebellion begins to recoil on him when the Percies, in league with Glendower of Wales and Douglas of Scotland, raise arms against him.

Meanwhile, Henry's son, Henry Prince of Wales, nicknamed Hal, adds to his father's distress by deserting the court for the taverns of Eastcheap, living among thieves and drunkards, and frequenting in particular the Boar's Head inn, dominated by the massive presence of Sir John Falstaff. Hal takes part in a robbery at Gadshill; but only to rob the robbers and later confront them – especially Falstaff – with their lies and cowardice. The money is repaid. In an interview with the king Hal promises reform.

The rebels, under the valiant, rash Harry Percy (Hotspur), finally meet the king in battle at Shrewsbury, but are defeated, due to betrayals and desertions. Hal saves his father from Douglas and defeats Hotspur in single combat. Falstaff – also in the battle but feigning death to escape injury – subsequently rises from his death-pose, gives Hotspur's corpse a new wound and claims, with Hal's consent, the victory as his own.

Part 2: Rebellion continues, led by the Archbishop of York, but again the rebels are weakened by defections. Falstaff is given a new commission and, saying farewell to Eastcheap, goes off to recruit soldiers in Gloucestershire, taking up quarters in the home of an old friend of his youth, Justice Shallow. These scenes provide the best comedy of either Part.

The rebels meet the king's forces, under Prince John, at Gaultree Forest, but, tricked by him into an amnesty, their leaders are hanged. Rebellion is finally suppressed, but the king immediately falls fatally sick. Before dying he is reconciled to his son. On becoming King Henry V, Hal announces his reform and banishes Falstaff.

SOURCES

Raphael Holinshed, *The Chronicles of England, Scotland, and Ireland . . . faithfully gathered & set forth* (1578; 2nd edition, 'newlie augmented', 1586).
Samuel Daniel, *The First Four Books of the Civil Wars between the two houses of Lancaster and York* (1595).
John Stow, *The Chronicles of England* (1580); and *The Annals of England* (1592).

PART ONE: TEXT

1 INTRODUCTION

Shakespeare's history plays are a unique national asset. There are ten of them in all, and eight of these are dedicated to a single continuous span of English history of about a century: from the end of the fourteenth to the end of the fifteenth century. In these plays medieval history is brought vividly alive. Shakespeare takes the turbulent period between the reigns of Richard II and Richard III – both ill-fated – and brings kings, queens and civil wars to a popular theatre audience. The series is not lacking in the serious analysis of history. It is a continuous study of men and women in the context of politics and political theory. It is this, and the broad diffusion of the dramatist's interests over a whole people, which makes it a series of history plays rather than tragedies. Here, undoubtedly, lies a major part of the enduring fascination of these plays: their depiction of events and people who are *remote* from the centres of power – the ordinary, and extraordinary, commoners of England.

National life is what Shakespeare presents: not only politicians and noblemen, but tradesmen, gardeners, prostitutes, foot-soldiers, bailiffs, scholars and conjurors.

Nowhere is this sense of a national epic more pronounced than in the two plays called *Henry IV*. Shakespeare creates a national panorama here which stretches from the court and its guilt-burdened, crisis-ridden king, to the seamy vital life of the London streets: the Boar's Head tavern, and the fat knight Sir John Falstaff. The plays open with a blight affecting the country: the moral blight of the murder of Richard II, the last in an unbroken line of sacred kings. They close anticipating national triumph in foreign wars under Henry IV's son, the warrior-king Henry V.

The present volume sets out to argue, here in Part One, that Shakespeare, in writing these history plays, was drawn to issues and themes which are most intrinsic to history: the issues of time, and of the interpretation (and distortion) of events. During the discussion, however, there is a gradual introduction of some of the hotly contested critical debates which the plays have provoked: debates which inevitably concentrate around the central figure of Prince Hal, the only participant in the plays who is poised between the two worlds of court and tavern.

The ensuing Part Two, on 'Performance', shows what light is thrown on these crucial issues by four widely differing interpretations in the theatre, and in conclusion a commitment to one of the four is made.

Deliberately omitted from the issues debated is any discussion of the barren topic of whether these *Henry IV* 'Parts' are one or two plays. It seems self-evident that they were written separately and each can – especially Part 1 – stand alone. It seems equally obvious that they are also a pair: that Part 2 is the natural and intended sequel to Part 1; and that there is a careful continuity of characters, themes and events between the two plays. There is surely no need to labour the issue any further.

2. The Making and Manufacturing of History

'Construing the times to their necessities'

'History' consists as much of interpretation as of bare facts. In some periods and places, interpretation actually comes to take precedence over fact. For the Elizabethans, as for modern totalitarian states, fact was so much subservient to interpretation that history became a form of mythology and propaganda. In the *Henry IV* plays, this becomes Shakespeare's theme. On the one hand, he faithfully transmits one of the central historical myths to which his age subscribed. On the other, he shows the events of Henry's reign being distorted even as they are made, according to local political necessity. He shows history being 'made', both in the sense of momentous things being done, and also in the sense of their falsification.

The 'central historical myth' which Shakespeare transmits is often called 'the *Tudor* myth'. It consists of interpreting the Tudors, of whom Elizabeth I was the last representative, as national saviours who rescued the country from a disastrous period of civil wars, spanning the period between the reigns of Richard II and Richard III. In this myth, the reign of Henry IV occupied a key position. It was he who committed the original crime. As Henry Bolingbroke, he seized and deposed Richard II, had him murdered and took his throne. In doing so, he destroyed centuries of rightful continuity.

To the Tudors, even more than to most monarchs, deposition seemed the blackest of political crimes. Threatened from abroad and by malcontents at home, aware that their own dynasty had been founded over the body of Richard III, it was deeply in their own interests to foster an ethic of unquestioning loyalty. Elizabeth's *Homilie against Disobedience and Wylfull Rebellion*, read in every church in the land, proclaimed that disloyalty to God's annointed monarch was a sin against the divine order itself. Royal propagandists stressed the sins of rebels, and how they were punished; and, time and again, it was Henry IV who featured in such lessons. Conversely, Elizabeth's enemies likewise looked to the past, and attempted to justify Henry – though they did so at some risk.

This Tudor myth, in which the reign of Henry IV holds such a key position, was given wide currency by Tudor historians, with the active encouragement and even the sponsorship of the Tudor monarchs. It was to these historians that Shakespeare went for source-material for his history-plays. It was a striking decision, because it was actually an unusual one. Undoubtedly, the official version of history enjoyed wide belief and support. The extent of the Elizabethan system of propaganda and censorship was matched only by the willingness of the public to be manipulated. Yet Shakespeare was almost alone among the Elizabethan dramatists in choosing the later Plantagenet period as his subject. Possibly, for most, the subject seemed too sensitive; the dangers of putting a foot wrong in interpreting it perhaps seemed too great. Whatever the reason, most history plays of the time were concerned either with foreign history, or with English history from a more remote period. Shakespeare's decision to devote eight plays to the vital period, from the reign of Richard II and the resulting national ills, through to the death of Richard III and the advent of the first of the Tudors, was unique. His interpretation of the period is almost wholly orthodox, nowhere more so than in his depiction of the reign of Henry IV. The historian Hall had called this 'the unquiet time'. Shakespeare follows suit. As will be seen, he construes Henry's reign in terms of a kind of curse, attendant on Richard's murder; with country and king afflicted by a malaise of rebellion and lawlessness.

Yet, as has already been said, even as he does so, he also creates his own comment on the manipulation of the truth for political ends. The characters of the two *Henry IV* plays constantly dispute the facts, or interpret them in widely different ways. 'Discrepant interpretation' has become part of the condition under which England exists, during Henry's guilty reign.

In effect, in *Henry IV*, every man becomes his own historian. None is reliable. In the preceding play, *Richard II*, there had been no shortage of trustworthy guides. The play was full of omens, commentators and prophets, and all were proved true. A Welsh captain is invented for a single short scene to describe the portents he has seen (whose warning is duly fulfilled):

> The bay trees in our country all are withered,
> And meteors fright the fixèd stars of heaven,
> The pale-faced moon looks bloody on the earth,
> And lean-looked prophets whisper fearful change.
> . . .   [II iv]

In *Henry IV*, there are no such things. This is the more noteworthy in that Shakespeare's main source, the account of the historian Holinshed, actually does contain an account of supernatural omens: 'In the moneth of March appeared a blasing starre, first betweene the east part of the firmament and the north, flashing foorth fire and flames round about it; and lastlie shooting foorth fierie beams towards the north; foreshewing (as was thought) the great effusion of bloud that followed, about the parts of Wales and Northumberland.' Shakespeare omits this; and where Holinshed gives credit to the story that the Welsh rebel Owen Glendower possessed magical powers, his claims are merely mocked in Shakespeare's play. The earth, Glendower boasts, shook at his birth and the sky blazed. Hotspur replies, 'Why, so it would have done / At the same season if your mother's cat / Had but kittened, though you yourself had never been born' [Part 1, III i 15–17].

In *Richard II*, even the humblest character seems gifted with political clairvoyance. A gardener, again invented for a single scene, compares King Richard's kingdom with an unweeded garden, and foretells his fall. More major figures spell out the constitutional or even the theological significance of events, at every turn. When Richard confiscates the estates that should have gone to Bolingbroke on his father's death, the Duke of York is on hand to point out the violation of the very principle by which Richard himself has come to the throne: 'for how art thou a king / But by fair sequence and succession' [II i]. Bolingbroke's father himself, John of Gaunt, had protested against Richard's leasing out of the country's land in terms almost of a sacrilege against 'this blessed plot, this earth, this realm, this England' [II i]. By contrast, in *Henry IV* Part 1 there is nobody to uphold the sacred integrity of the kingdom, when the rebels sit down to plan how the country is to be split after, as they hope, they have overthrown the king. We may suspect their plan to be a wrong against the country, but there is no-one in the play to tell us so. In the new, fallen, secular world of Henry IV's reign, neither king nor country possesses its former sacredness. There are no upholders left, to protest that rebellion is a crime against God; to compare it with Golgotha, Pilate or Judas; or to prophesy God's punishment against the offenders, as in *Richard II*. Political right and wrong have become a matter of opinion. King and rebels seem to possess an equal righteousness. Right and wrong are largely decided by the event.

An even more telling indication of the condition of England under Bolingbroke/Henry IV is that facts themselves are now disputed. Early in Part 1 the first clash between the king and the men who are to become his enemies provides us with an example. The scene is a council debate concerning prisoners of war. Hotspur, having taken prisoners on the king's behalf in his wars against the Scots, now apparently refuses to hand them over. The king in his turn refuses to ransom Hotspur's cousin Mortimer, taken prisoner in the king's wars against the Welsh.

Hotspur defends himself with energy. The royal agent who claimed his prisoners was an effeminate fop, who, in the height of battle, 'as the soldiers bore dead bodies by', 'called them untaught knaves, unmannerly, / To bring a slovenly unhansome corpse / Betwixt the wind and his nobility' [1, I iii 41–4]. Hotspur, not surprisingly, had given him no very polite reply. It is not clear, even if we accept Hotspur's story uncritically, who is in the right. Is the king only claiming what is his own? Is it usual for the king to demand captured prisoners from his captains? Or is it so *un*usual as to be provocative? We do not know. We are not told.

As to the king's refusal to ransom Mortimer: this is still more problematic. The grounds for his refusal are his claim that Mortimer had, instead of fighting, capitulated to Glendower; or, worse still, actually sold out to the enemy. It is a charge which Hotspur angrily denies, claiming rather that Mortimer fought a mighty battle, in personal combat with Owen Glendower himself – an encounter which he describes, in heroic terms:

> Three times they breathed, and three times did they drink,
> Upon agreement, of swift Severn's flood,
> Who then affrighted with their bloody looks
> Ran fearfully among the trembling reeds,
> And hid his crisp head in the hollow bank,
> Blood-stainèd with these valiant combatants.
>
> [1, I iii 92–106]

Henry does not reply in detail. He simply denies every word: 'Thou does belie him, Percy, thou dost bely him, / He never did encounter with Glendower.' The discrepancy is astounding and is not resolved. The incident is never again referred to in the play. We see Mortimer and Glendower together, later in the play, and Mortimer has become Glendower's son-in-law. Yet this is not proof that they never fought. Quite simply, we do not know. Hotspur's account is suspiciously highly-coloured; and after all he was three hundred miles away at the time of the fight he describes so intimately. Henry, on the other hand, has excellent reasons for branding Mortimer a traitor. Mortimer had been 'proclaimed, / By Richard that dead is, the next of blood' [143–4]. His title to the throne was stronger than Henry's own. Small wonder that Henry should vilify him, and seek to diminish the threat he represented. For us, as audience, the problem of arbitrating between flat contradictions, so vehemently upheld on either side, is insoluble. Nor does our task become any easier as the play progresses. The only hints we receive seem to suggest that, if anything, both sides are in the wrong.

Act IV scene i of Part 1 finds the rebels reckoning up their forces against the king. Their numbers are depleted. Hotspur's father, Northumberland, has sent news that he is sick (*'crafty-sick'*, as it turns out) and cannot bring his troops. Worcester laments this, less on account of the depletion of their overall forces, than because of the doubt it throws on their cause:

> And think how such an apprehension
> May turn the tide of fearful faction,
> And breed a kind of question in our cause.
> For well you know we of the offering side
> Must keep aloof from strict arbitrement,
> And stop all sight-holes, every loop from whence
> The eye of reason may pry in upon us.   [IV i 66–72]

A cause which cannot bear the scrutiny of reason must be suspect; and when, in delegations between the two camps, the grievances of the rebels are to be spelled out, they are notable for their vagueness. There is a continual retreat, in these accounts, to Henry's earlier sins as Bolingbroke: his exceeding the terms on which Northumberland and Worcester had offered their friendship; taking on himself the redressing of grievances; deposing and killing the king; and assuming the crown himself. These complaints are made by Hotspur to the king's representative Sir Walter Blunt [IV iii], and subsequently repeated by Worcester to the king's face [v i]. Each time, however, the tale becomes weaker as it reaches recent events. The king, Hotspur declares, 'Broke oath on oath, committed wrong on wrong, / And in conclusion drove us to seek out / This head of safety' [IV iii 101–3]. The accusation is conspicuously lame. Worcester flees for the safety of metaphor:

And being fed by us, you used us so
As that ungentle gull the cuckoo's bird
Useth the sparrow – did oppress our nest,
Grew by our feeding to so great a bulk
That even our love durst not come near your sight
For fear of swallowing. But with nimble wing
We were enforced for safety sake to fly
Out of your sight, and raise this present head. [v i 59–66]

When the king offers truce and friendship, Worcester, returning to his own camp, disguises the fact from Hotspur, so making
war a certainty. Again it looks as if he fears that his case cannot
stand the scrutiny of reason.

Yet the king too has his fears about the weakness of his cause;
and, like Worcester, he half-confesses as much. In the
reconciliation-scene between him and his son and heir Prince
Hal, Henry dwells at some length on his political arts during
King Richard's reign, all leading up to the theft of the crown.
His son – he believes – shows no sign of possessing the same
astuteness; and, in a manner typical of critical fathers, Henry
makes an invidious comparison between his own dissolute son
and his far abler contemporary, the warrior Hotspur:

              For all the world
As thou art to this hour was Richard then
When I from France set foot at Ravenspurg,
And even as I was then is Percy now.
Now, by my sceptre, and my soul to boot,
He hath more worthy interest to the state
Than thou the shadow of succession.
For of no right, nor colour like to right,
He doth fill fields with harness in the realm.
                 [III ii 93–101]

The speech contains an interesting admission. Hotspur comes
closer than Hal to the image of Hal's father, *because* Hotspur,
like Henry, has 'no right, nor colour like to right' on his side.
Not until Part 2 does Henry make an open admission of his
political sins. Here, however, is the next best thing, and the
inadvertent confession does much to confirm the rebels'
accusations.

Appropriately, at the start of Part 2 the introductory Chorus is *'Rumour, painted full of tongues'*. Rumour operates in a country whose populace has become a 'wavering multitude' [Induction, line 19]. With contending factions, both equally in the wrong, public opinion is easily misled. Distortion replaces truth. The processes are initiated by the king and his rebel peers. Early in Part 1, Hotspur had drastically reinterpreted the reign of King Richard, so as to dignify Richard at Henry's expense. If, looking back, the reign of Richard seemed good, the crime of deposition could be thrown in Henry's face. So, though Richard's reign was in fact disastrous for the nation, he becomes, in Hotspur's distorted memory, 'Richard, that sweet lovely rose' [1, ɪ iii 173].

The mob, in Part 2, follows suit. The rebellion here is led by the Archbishop of York, and this in itself is a marked change from the former reign, in which bishops would stand up, at the cost of their own lives, to defend the divine right of kings and prophesy ruin to usurpers. This prelate describes the populace as a 'common dog, [which] didst . . . disgorge / Thy glutton bosom of the royal Richard – / And now thou wouldst eat thy dead vomit up' [ɪ iii 97–9]. His rebellion depends on this in part for its chances of success. Nevertheless, it is partly in lament that he immediately asks, 'What trust is in these times?' Worcester's distrust of the king's offer of a truce, in Part 1, is largely justified in Part 2, where the archbishop foolishly accepts a truce from the king's side, and promptly loses his life. The pact offered by Prince John was for the redress of general grievances. The archbishop takes this offer to include a general amnesty. He is mistaken. Technically, Prince John breaks no vow. He only breaks his good faith. The 'small print' of the agreement becomes, like every other issue of politics in either play, a matter for dispute, according to factional advantage. It is presumably this that Westmoreland, the prince's emissary, means when he urges his enemies to 'construe the times to their necessities'! [2, ɪv i 102]

3 'The Book of Fate': Henry's Blighted Reign

In Part 2, as Henry awaits the outcome of the latest rebellion against him – the archbishop's – he thinks about the turmoil which has characterised his reign. He arrives at the conclusion that, had he been able to foresee the future, he could never have faced such consequences as his actions entailed. His speech on the 'book of fate' opens with what sounds like a craving for foreknowledge, but rapidly fills with weary despair:

> O God, that one might read the book of fate,
> And see the revolution of the times
> Make mountains level, and the continent,
> Weary of solid firmness, melt itself
> Into the sea; and other times to see
> The beachy girdle of the ocean
> Too wide for Neptune's hips; how chance's mocks
> And changes fill the cup of alteration
> With divers liquors! O, if this were seen,
> The happiest youth, viewing his progress through,
> What perils past, what crosses to ensue,
> Would shut the book and sit him down and die.
>
> [2, iii i 45ff.; last 3½ ll. in Q only]

Time, in this speech, is a destructive, even a malicious, mocking agency. Man is not the only casualty, but exists in a context of global desolation; of solid things erased or dissolved. At best, the processes of change seem whimsical, as in the image of the ill-fitting girdle. At worst, man himself is the victim of a perverse experimentation in the 'cup of alteration' by which his fate fluctuates. The youth remaining innocent of the future remains happy. Knowledge of it is lethal.

Henry then reviews his own past. Still protesting his own innocence, that he was forced to assume the crown ('I and greatness were compelled to kiss'), he sees himself as a passive victim of bewildering change. First, Northumberland was Richard's friend. Then 'they were at wars'. Then Northumberland was Henry's own friend, but now – . Clearly, to Henry, the 'revolution of the times' seems a subversive cycle in which he is imprisoned. Referring to the prophecies which Richard

uttered before his death [*R. II* v i 55–68], and which now seem
to be fulfilled (of Northumberland's future treachery to Henry
and of the advent of civil war), Henry sees himself as a prisoner
of time. He feels himself to be a figure in a preordained and
inescapable sequence of events. Warwick, so often a comforter,
tries to reassure him by arguing that Richard simply made a
good guess, knowing what kind of a man Northumberland was.
Henry, however, ignores Warwick's argument, and attends
instead to one of the metaphors Warwick had used: of weak
beginnings growing to be 'the hatch and brood of time'. It is a
metaphor, of course, of the hatching of eggs. What Warwick
had meant was that, by seeing an egg, a man might guess that a
chicken would follow. To the king, however, the metaphor
seems to indicate unstoppable growth, and his conclusion
remains deterministic: 'Are these things, then, necessities?' His
only positive response is to '*meet* them like necessities'. There is
no mistaking, however, Henry's fatalistic view of time and his
own role in it. As he has sown, so he reaps. His reign is blighted
by the curse of deposition, and is doomed to work the curse out.

It is here that the metaphor of disease assumes such
significance. Sickness of any kind is hardly mentioned in Part 1.
In Part 2, however, it is rife. We begin with Northumberland's
illness and all its trappings. In the next scene we hear that the
king himself is sick. Once introduced, the fact is mentioned in
numerous dialogues. In the following scene, it crops up again,
when the archbishop and his allies, in the middle of plotting
against him, refer to Henry as 'the unfirm King' [i iii 73], with
the suggestion of illness as well as insecurity. Furthermore, the
archbishop goes on, as already seen, to speak of the country's
nausea, of a commonwealth 'sick of their own choice', and
wishing to discharge their stomachs of him, as they once did of
Richard. In Act ii, Hal, in his scene with Poins, again keeps us
in mind of his father's illness. And when, eventually, we see the
king [iii i], there is very strong stress laid on the sickness of king
and country. The king's illness involves sleeplessness, as he
tells us in the famous speech, on sleep, 'Uneasy lies the head
that wears a crown'. This line, and the king's recognition that
he has 'frighted' sleep away, convey the idea that his sickness is
not merely accidental and physical, but also partly moral. It is
a disease which afflicts other guilty men in other Shakes-

pearean plays, from Richard III to Macbeth. The king then
immediately transfers the idea of sickness from the physical
body to the 'body politic':

> Then you perceive the body of our kingdom
> How foul it is, what rank diseases grow,
> And with what danger, near the heart of it. [2, III i 38–40]

Warwick replies, comfortingly, that,

> It is but as a body yet distempered,
> Which to his former strength may be restored
> With good advice and little medicine,   [41–3]

but Henry, in his 'book of fate' speech implicitly denies
Warwick's comfort, by quoting Richard's prophecy,

> 'The time will come that foul sin, gathering head,
> Shall break into corruption' – so went on,
> Foretelling this same time's condition,
> And the division of our amity.   [72–5]

It is a theme taken up again by the archbishop, presenting the
case for rebellion to Westmoreland:

>   we are all diseased,
> And with our surfeiting and wanton hours
> Have brought ourselves into a burning fever,
> And we must bleed for it; of which disease
> Our late King Richard being infected, died.   [IV i 54–8]

He adds that, though he does not set up as a physician – in other
words, he has no pretensions himself to the crown – he
nevertheless hopes, with his show of force, to 'diet rank minds
sick of happiness, / And purge th' obstructions which begin to
stop / Our very veins of life'. His attempt, of course, fails – as
indeed it must. His rebellion cannot be a cure: it is a symptom
of the original disease. Neither can the kingdom be cleansed
merely by his defeat. As if to stress this, the reports of the defeat
of this last rebellion, when they reach Henry in Act IV scene iv,
only make him more sick. It is the last phase of Henry's stricken

reign, and his son's diagnosis, just before his father's death, is that the crown has been a kind of consuming disease, which has finally wasted him completely:

> 'Therefore thou best of gold art worse than gold.
> Other, less fine in carat, is more precious,
> Preserving life in medicine potable;
> But thou, most fine, most honoured, most renowned,
> Hast eat thy bearer up.' . . .   [IV v 161–5]

Only when the whole process is completed with Henry's death, and the curse is lifted from his successor, can Hal, acceding to the crown, at last apply an image of health to the country, when he urges,

> let us choose such limbs of noble counsel,
> That the great body of our state may go
> In equal rank with the best-governed nation.   [v ii 135–7]

His own 'tide of blood', having formerly 'flowed in vanity', now ebbs into the 'state of floods'. This last phrase seems to mean, the general tide of a state's existence. His own personal health, in other words, will be at one with the good health of his country. It will flow in 'formal majesty'. All the previous wild imagery of fever will cease, with the death of Henry IV, who has 'gone wild into his grave' [v ii 123], taking with him the whole sickness of the country.

The sickness theme is greatly reinforced in the scenes involving Falstaff. As has long been recognised, even though Falstaff's sphere of life is apparently remote from the concerns of statecraft, he is nevertheless designed by Shakespeare as a kind of parody-counterpart of King Henry. As such, he reflects the king's basic state of health or sickness. He even provides an ironic comment on the king's profession. Falstaff only directly impersonates the king on one occasion [1, II iv], and only once appears in the same scene as the king (before the battle of Shrewsbury, at the end of Part 1), but the parallels are nevertheless very strong.

Basically, Falstaff echoes in comedy form the king's pattern of growth, followed by decline. First, however, there is the parallel between their occupations. Theft is Falstaff's. It is his vocation, and, as he tells Hal, "'tis no sin for a man to labour in his vocation' [1, I ii 104–5]. The king, too, being a usurper, is a thief. The closest the king comes himself to acknowledging this is in conceding to Hal that 'It *seemed* in me / But as an honour snatched with boisterous hand' [2, IV v 190–1]; or, in the corresponding scene in Part 1, that 'I did *pluck* allegiance from men's hearts' [III ii 52]. Mostly, he and his son speak rather of 'winning' the crown than stealing it. His enemies are less reticent. Worcester, in delivering the cause of his rebellion before the battle of Shrewsbury, accuses Henry: 'You took occasion to be quickly wooed / To gripe the general sway into your hand' [1, v i 56–7]. Hotspur, in an earlier scene, had spoken of Henry robbing King Richard of life as well as crown [1, IV iii 91]. It is intriguing that, at the end of Part 2, Hal, prematurely believing his father to be dead, takes away his crown. It is an act which Henry construes as theft: 'Thou hast stolen that which after some few hours / Were thine without offence' [2, IV v 102–3]. Like Falstaff, Hal mimicks Henry's offence. What, in Falstaff's case, makes the parallel particularly strong is the Gadshill episode. Here, Falstaff's robbery of the travellers is immediately followed by his being robbed in turn by his own friends. This is at least the aim of the king's former allies in the usurpation, the Percy faction.

Even in his most striking and principal characteristic, however, Falstaff parallels Henry. Sir John is above all fat; a 'stuffed cloak-bag of guts', who 'lards the lean earth as he walks along'. The king cannot match this; except metaphorically. Here, at least, he is depicted as Falstaff's equal. In the third scene of Part 1, the remark by Worcester which provokes his dismissal from the chamber is:

> Our house, my sovereign liege, little deserves
> The scourge of greatness to be used on it,
> And that same greatness too which our own hands
> Have holp to make so portly.   [1, I iii 10–13]

The same character develops the idea, in the recrimination-scene before Shrewsbury, into the incongruous image of the over-fed cuckoo:

> you used us so
> As that ungentle gull the cuckoo's bird
> Useth the sparrow – did oppress our nest,
> Grew by our feeding to so great a bulk
> That even our love durst not come near your sight
> For fear of swallowing. . . .   [1, v i 59–64]

This portliness is, however, followed – with both men – by a period of decline. In Part 2, there is a recurrent stress on disease, and on a wasting process both physical and financial. Together with sickness, one of the most consistently recurring images in the plays is that of swelling and gorging; but always with its accompanying images of surfeit, purging, disgorging or wasting away. Falstaff is in both plays contrasted with his pitifully-thin band of recruits in the wars. Henry speaks of King Richard's over-exposure to the public in terms of being 'daily swallowed by men's eyes', to the point of 'surfeit', until they were 'glutted, gorged and full' [1, iii ii 70, 71, 84]. Rebellion on the other hand engenders 'moody beggars, starving for a time / Of pell-mell havoc and confusion' [1, v i 81–2]. In this world of evident predatoriness, where 'advantage feeds him fat while men delay' [1, iii ii end], Falstaff personifies the national condition, preying upon travellers, upon the Hostess, and finally on Justice Shallow: 'if the young dace be a bait for the old pike, I see no reason in the law of nature but I may snap at him' [2, iii ii end]. However, physically, Sir John is in decline. From the first sight of him in Part 2, there is a constant stress on his diseases and his age. For the first time, his companions begin to think and speak of him as a 'withered elder' [ii iv]. The same word is applied to the king; or rather, he applies it to himself. Care has worn the shell of his body 'so thin, that life looks through and will break out' [iv iv 120], and he speaks of how 'health . . . is flown / From this bare withered trunk' [iv v 227–8]. In both cases, the wasting process is financial as well as physical. With Falstaff it is a 'consumption of the purse; borrowing only lingers it out, but the disease is incurable' [i ii end]. In the next scene, the king's coffers are said to 'sound / With hollow poverty and emptiness' [i iii 75); and of course the king has long been spoken of as a debtor, politically ('The king is kind, and well we know the king / Knows at what time to promise, when to pay' [1, iv iii 52–3]).

Even in the idea of repentance, Falstaff parallels the king. He is, of course, incorrigible; but, preposterously, he does on one occasion swear, 'Well, I'll repent' [1, III iii 4]. He echoes, here, the king's forever unfulfilled dream of leading a crusade, to 'draw no swords but what are sanctified' and to die in Jerusalem.

Since the king still wears the crown, he is never able to absolve himself from the guilt of stealing it. Instead, he sickens and decays, and in every detail of his progress, Falstaff is present as a parody-equivalent. Thief, debtor, swollen; but sick and wasting, unable to shed his guilt; he represents the kingdom's imprisonment in the crime of its king.

4   'REDEEMING TIME': HAL'S 'VIRTUE' AND CONTRAST WITH FALSTAFF AND HOTSPUR

Alone of all the characters in the two plays, Prince Hal has a justified optimism about his ability to control the future. In speaking at all of the future, Hal is unusual. This is a reign in which both king and rebels insistently rake over the grievances of the past. This is as pronounced at the end of Part 2 as it was at the beginning of Part 1, with the rebel Mowbray's speech of grievance [2, IV i]. His hatred dates back to the time when his father, in effect acting as Richard II's champion, was challenged to combat by Henry, the then Henry Bolingbroke [*R.II*, I i]. Mowbray's speech gives no very cogent account of his grievances. He seems to hate Henry because his father hated him, no more. Time and again, however, it is to this remoter period that men's minds turn, repeatedly harking back to Bolingbroke's banishment after the tournament at which he was to have met the elder Mowbray; his banishment; his return to claim his rights; and the early stages of his overthrow of Richard. The impression of the force which these events exert in the drama is enhanced by the plays' concentration on action which is derived from the past, and related to rebellion. On the ordinary business of Henry's reign, they are silent.

Prince Hal, however, repeatedly speaks, not in the past, but in the future tense. It is a characteristic noticeable even in his first appearance in the plays, in the final speech of Act I scene ii of Part 1. This is the famous 'I know you all' speech; a soliloquy in which Hal announces that he no more than tolerates his present low company. Already, his mind is firmly fixed on the future; on the miraculous transformation with which he plans to dazzle the world. He concludes,

> I'll so offend, to make offence a skill,
> Redeeming time when men think least I will.

Which of the two meanings of the word 'redeem' is uppermost here – the act of salvation, or the rescue of an article from pawn – may be debatable; but what Hal intends, in effect, amounts to the 'salvation' of time. It is more than a matter of making up for the period he will spend in waste and riot. The word he chooses indicates an act of release, and the choice is significant. In his father's reign – during the whole of which Hal will play truant – the present will be the prisoner of the past. Ancient grievances haunt the usurper. His reign inexorably enacts the curse of the king he deposed. When Hal becomes Henry v, however, time will be released and the curse of the past lifted. Hal is therefore given in these plays a unique relationship with the future, as saviour and redeemer. The terminology may seem strange, when applied to an Eastcheap reveller, but it will be argued that Hal's addiction to low life is by no means a straightforward matter.

On two major occasions, Hal overtly refers to his possession of a scheme for the future. These occasions are the reconciliation-scenes with his father, one in each play. In the first, the king begins, as usual by casting his mind back to the past: 'I know not whether God will have it so / For some displeasing service *I have done*, / That, in his secret doom out of my blood / He'll breed revengement and a scourge for me . . .' [1, III ii 4–7]. It is the usual view of present time as a punishment for past sins. By the end of the scene, however, Hal has turned the argument round to the future:

> I will redeem all this on Percy's head,
> And in the closing of some glorious day

> Be bold to tell you that I am your son,
>
> . . .
>
> for the time will come
> That I shall make this northern youth exchange
> His glorious deeds for my indignities.   [132–4, 144–6]

It is a speech which uses the future tense, of 'shall' and 'will',
over a dozen times. The corresponding scene in Part 2 is rather
less strident – Hal's father is after all on the point of death.
Nevertheless, it contains very similar material; the same
reference to the purposed change to come, and the vow to
defend the crown which his father has won for him,

> Which I with more than with a common pain
> 'Gainst all the world will rightfully maintain.
>
> [2, IV v 222–3]

Alone of any man in the play, Prince Hal's plans for the future
are actually fulfilled. In Part 1, the rebels are, together with the
rest of the country, infected with a physical and moral malaise.
Hotspur's father Northumberland feigns sickness and with-
draws from the rebellion: his defection 'doth infect / The very
life-blood of our enterprise' [IV i 28–9]. Percy's battle-cry is
'Esperance' – 'Hope' – but his hopes prove mocking. In his
death speech, he sees himself as 'time's fool': the victim and
slave of the processes of destiny. At the end his plans are broken
and, like so many others in the play, even his final awareness of
his failure gives him no insight into the inscrutable forces of
time and destiny themselves. He feels he 'could prophesy', but
'the earthy and cold hand of death / Lies on my tongue'. The
corresponding rebellion in Part 2 goes the same way. Lord
Bardolph speaks confidently of plotting the future, using the
analogy of an architect's plans. His extended simile is of
surveying, testing the foundations, making drawings and
models, and costing. These low-key rebels are evidently
anxious not to repeat Hotspur's rash trusting to hope alone. Yet
they are no more successful than he was. Their plans for the
future are just as comprehensively destroyed. Once again there
is a failed prophet among their number: Hastings, who
prophesies that civil war will have no end. He is wrong.
   At least part of Hal's function by the end of Part 2, when he

succeeds to the throne, is 'To *frustrate* prophecies, and to raze
out / Rotten opinion' [v ii 127–8]. In place of the infected past,
and of erroneous views of the future, comes Hal's redemption of
his country, and of time itself. The theme anticipates the death
of Macbeth, when, for the first time, 'the time is free'.

The interim, however, has been for Hal a period when time
was almost suspended. He awaits the time when his destiny
comes under his control, and time can progress. Until then,
time enters a kind of hibernation, and, for the exact duration of
his father's reign, Hal is placed in Eastcheap, removed from
contact with power. Clearly, part of the reason for this is so that
Hal will be untainted by the curse which blights his father's
tenure of the crown. It is significant that, when trickery is
necessary to defeat the archbishop's rebellion in Part 2, it is not
Hal but his brother Prince John who is given the task.

The problem is, whether it is also necessary to argue, as
many critics have always done, that Hal's residence in
Eastcheap is also constructive: a process of education, as well as
a means of refuge. The usual theory is that Hal here learns
about the common people, an experience he later puts to use in
his abilities as a leader of men in *Henry V*.

There is, in fact, only one speech in either play to support
such an interpretation. It comes shortly before King Henry's
death. The king laments his son's prodigality, and foretells –
another *false* prophecy – the future ruin of his kingdom. It is
Warwick who tries to comfort the king by making the bravest
interpretation of Hal's behaviour;

> My gracious lord, you look beyond him quite.
> The prince but studies his companions
> Like a strange tongue, wherein, to gain the language,
> 'Tis needful that the most immodest word
> Be looked upon and learnt, which once attained,
> Your highness knows, comes to no further use
> But to be known and hated. . . .   [2, IV iv 67–73]

Even this interpretation is however notable more for its oddity
than its plausibility; it turns out in fact to be an image of
uselessness rather than of constructiveness. Loose behaviour is
a language to be learned. But, once learned, it will be discarded
and loathed.

In one sense, however, Warwick's diagnosis is correct. Hal does experience loathing for Eastcheap. Where Warwick is wrong is in believing that this is something which must be learned by diligent study. All the learning Hal needs, he already possesses at the opening of Part 1. He *knows* them all, already, as he tells us; and will tolerate them for a while.

In one view of the play, there is never any sense of Hal enjoying his life in Eastcheap; or at least there are only rare moments of pleasure, and always when Hal is enjoying a practical joke at his companions' expense. The Gadshill incident is an example. Even as a practical joker, Hal sometimes reveals his distate. One incident links up with Warwick's analogy of the foreign language. This incident is Hal's joke at the expense of Francis the waiter. It is a joke which exploits the victim's limited vocabulary, and his catch-phrase 'Anon anon sir' in particular. Clearly this tavern-language is one which Hal despises. He says he is proficient in it in a mere quarter-of-an-hour. Those who live by it he evidently regards as hardly human ('That ever this fellow should have fewer words than a parrot, and yet the son of a woman!'), and the joke is indeed Pavlovian. There is no mistaking Hal's contempt for the man whose devotion he enjoys, as he traps him with his inadequacy and then proceeds to baffle him by his own inventiveness with words. This is Hal rather self-consciously sounding 'the very bass string of humility' [1, II iv 6]. Similarly in Part 2, Hal openly despises even his accomplice in the Francis trick, Poins: 'What a disgrace is it to me to remember thy name! or to know thy face tomorrow! or to take note how many pairs of silk stockings thou hast – viz. these, and those that were thy peach-coloured once!' [2, II ii 12–16]

We may note that, while in theory he is committed to a life of riot in Eastcheap, and earns the reputation of a dissolute life, we never actually see him in this character. He lives in taverns but never drinks. He never touches a woman. He once proposes a theft, but only to demonstrate how brief is Falstaff's vow of reformation. When Falstaff accepts the idea with alacrity, and invites Hal to join in the fun, Hal is almost shocked: 'Who I? Rob? I a thief? Not I, by my faith.' He joins in the Gadshill escapade only in order to rob the robbers. Later, he repays the theft with interest. We hear of his boxing the ears of the Lord

Chief Justice [2, 1 ii], but the incident is kept off-stage. In fact, in Part 2, Hal's contact with low-life is limited to one encounter, far less than in Part 1. Even that is marked by the same pronounced sense of a man aware he is demeaning himself, since he dwells on this fact, as in the Francis scene. The circumstances are fairly similar, though this time Hal and Poins actually impersonate waiters, in order to spy on Falstaff. In the last speech of Act II scene ii of Part 2, Hal spells out his humiliation:

> From a god to a bull? a heavy declension! It was Jove's case. From a prince to a prentice? A low transformation, that shall be mine; for in everything the purpose must weigh with the folly.

In this last revealing remark, he indicates that for him riot and folly are a purpose, not a pleasure. Again, the impression is of a distasteful necessity. Only twice does Hal deviate from his course of a planned waste of time. Once in each play, he is called to action against the rebels. In Part 1, at the end of Act III ('The land is burning, Percy stands on high, / And either they or we must lower lie'), Hal proceeds to give the world a foretaste of his eventual transformation by his deeds at the battle of Shrewsbury. He is forced to do so simply in order to protect the inheritance for which he is waiting. Similarly, in Part 2 (though this time we do not see him in action), he is stirred at the end of Act II to defend his father's tenure of the crown which is to be his own: 'By heaven, Poins, I feel me much to blame, / So idly to profane the precious time / When tempest of commotion, like the south / Borne with black vapour, doth begin to melt / And drop upon our bare unarmèd heads.' With these two very practical exceptions, Hal has deliberately suspended active time while his father lives. As his instant transformation into a brilliant soldier demonstrates, at Shrewsbury, he is already fully prepared for kingship: his future identity is already there, fully formed and spectacular. The usefulness of Eastcheap is that it provides the best possible disguise of this fact, while Hal waits for his time to arrive.

Interestingly, the other character who uses the vocabulary of redemption in relation to time is Harry Hotspur. In the

historical sources, Hotspur was aged 39 at his death; Hal was
nearly 16. Shakespeare alters their ages so that the two men
may emerge as contemporaries and rivals. Hotspur's version of
redeeming time is not, however, identical with Hal's. It centres
on the theme of honour:

> No, yet time serves wherein you may redeem
> Your banished honours, and restore yourselves
> Into the good thoughts of the world again:
> Revenge the jeering and disdained contempt
> Of this proud King, who studies day and night
> To answer all the debt he owes to you
> Even with the bloody payment of your deaths.
>   [1, I iii 178–83]

This speech, with its first mention in either play of Henry IV as a
bad debtor, is spoken to Worcester and Northumberland,
urging them to action against Henry. But Hotspur rapidly
moves into a kind of soliloquy, in which his imagination leads
him to conceive impossible exploits in the name of honour:

> To pluck bright honour from the pale-faced moon,
> Or dive into the bottom of the deep,
> Where fathom-line could never touch the ground,
> And pluck up drownèd honour by the locks,
> So he that doth redeem her thence might wear
> Without corrival all her dignities.   [199–204]

It is an extraordinary and evocative speech, and the language
of redemption seems appropriate to the mystical concept of
heroism he is straining to describe. It is noticeable that time is
here a subservient factor. Where Hal spoke of redeeming time,
Hotspur speaks only of time serving to redeem honour.
Accordingly, Hotspur is characterised by the urgency and
impatience with which he pursues his personal goal; and by the
imaginative leaps he makes towards it, contracting time and
space.

> O gentlemen, the time of life is short!
> To spend that shortness basely were too long
> If life did ride upon a dial's point,
> Still ending at the arrival of an hour.

> And if we live, we live to tread on kings,
> If die, brave death, when princes die with us!
> . Now, for our consciences, the arms are fair
> When the intent of bearing them is just.
>
> [1, v ii 81–8]

Hotspur may end the play as 'time's fool', yet still the words 'valour', 'honour', 'chivalry' cling to him, and his widow has our assent when, in Part 2, she describes him, 'O wondrous him! / O miracle of men!' [ii iii 32–3]. Shakespeare's portrayal of Hotspur swings continually between fool and hero. In the first Act of Part 1, raging against 'this vile politician, Bolingbroke', he is 'a wasp-stung and impatient fool' [i iii 233]. When he is crossing Glendower, or making himself believe that the desertion of his allies is on the whole a good thing, we see the mad-cap rather than the hero. Yet, within the play he inspires affectionate tolerance (from, say, Blunt [in i iii]; or from Glendower himself) which guides our own ultimate attitude to him. More than this, he inspires love. We see Hotspur, as we do not see Hal, in an affectionate domestic context. The scenes with his wife, with their rough tenderness, are an actor's gift, and do much to sway our sympathies in his favour; a feeling almost of protectiveness, which is indeed enhanced when he is manipulated by Worcester or betrayed by his own father. Since he and Hal are directly compared, his impatience with time, his determination to make it serve the cause of honour, constitute a notable challenge to Hal's patient planning of a time to come. He is depicted as a man incapable of 'playing a part' and his hot blood inspires a warmth of affection which never seems to attach to Hal. His innocence discredits wiser men.

The other notable challenger to Hal's handling of time in these plays is Falstaff. For Falstaff, the only permissible use of time is waste. He is quite immune to serious purpose. His famous dismissal of honour [Part 1, v i] is the best-known example, but there are many others. At the end of Act iii in the first play, where Hal begins to warm to the emergency ('The land is burning . . .'), Falstaff seems momentarily to be caught up in the enthusiasm: 'Rare words! Brave world!'. Immediately, however, he reverts to type: 'Hostess, my breakfast, come! / O, I could wish this tavern were my drum.' Similarly,

in Part 2, Falstaff is again called to war [II iv]. He says his manly
farewells to the ladies, and they are moved to tears as their hero
departs, perhaps never to return: 'Well, fare thee well. I have
known thee these twenty-nine years, come peascod-time, but
an honester and truer-hearted man – well, fare thee well.'
However, true to form, Falstaff immediately spoils the effect by
sending back an urgent summons for Doll Tearsheet. Once
again the flesh overwhelms the spirit.

Part of the piquancy of Falstaff's preposterous cowardice is
that he *can* actually fight. Shallow remembers him as 'a good
backsword man'; he is certainly a better man than Pistol, and
the rebel Coleville surrenders to him on sight. However,
self-preservation always comes first. As Poins predicts, at
Gadshill he fights no 'longer than he sees reason'.

It is interesting, then, that Shakespeare is determined to
include a figure like Falstaff in the serious battle-scenes of both
plays, giving him major speeches and substantial comic action.
The effect of this is that Falstaff very effectively deflates
seriousness. Lying doggo – but very much alive – alongside the
corpse of Hotspur, he listens to Hal's rather pompous eulogy
and to his plans for funeral preparations, and then produces the
best comic moment of the play when Hal leaves, rising
indignantly from the dead at the idea of being 'Embowelled!'
Here his comic resurrection tends to debunk Hotspur's serious
death. Earlier, it is Hal who is the victim of his jokes. As Hal
meets him on the battlefield, begging a weapon from him, he is
handed Falstaff's pistol case, and finds a bottle of sack inside it.
The unspoken answer to Hal's furious exit-line, 'What, is it a
time to jest and dally now?' must be 'yes'. For Falstaff, time is
not sacred; to be redeemed, or to be enlisted to redeem honour.
To him, nothing is sacred. Time is to be wasted (though of
course life must be preserved); and the prominence given to his
very persuasive view of time does, like Hotspur's, compel us to
make a comparison with Hal's. The comparison is not
necessarily in Hal's favour.

5 'THE FATHER RUFFIAN', 'THE TIDE OF BLOOD': 1, II iv

Discussion of Prince Hal's approach to time, compared with that of either Hotspur or Falstaff, immediately and inevitably leads on to the play's most persistent critical issue: of Hal's coldness or calculation.

With Hal making so early an announcement that he knows and places his tavern-companions, and will one day shed them and be transformed, there is the strongest temptation to take the announcement as a kind of scheming. It may not necessarily be. It should be noted that a quite different kind of explanation is possible. This would be, to explain the speech in terms of dramaturgic convenience, with Shakespeare simply trying to signal to his audience what pattern of events to look for. Nevertheless, this kind of shorthand clearly has its attendant risks in terms of the kind of character-comment it invites. Much will depend, in production, on whether a director wishes to emphasise this speech's suggestions of cold-blooded scheming, or whether he can contrive to 'lose' them.

The whole issue of coldness is related to that of Hal's paternity. Not that there is any doubt that Hal is genetically the son of Henry IV. The play contains, however, an additional father-figure in the shape of Falstaff. The quality of allegiance Hal bears to either father is the subject of varying interpretation by all three men, and of course by innumerable literary critics.

This issue receives significant impetus early on in Part 1 [II iv]. This is one of the play's tavern-scenes which, in its considerable length, covers first the Francis episode, then the aftermath of the Gadshill robbery, then finally a mock play on the subject of Henry IV, reproving his son (an anticipation of the real scene between the king and Hal in III ii). It is a scene which features Falstaff in his most outrageous, winning style; yet it clearly prefigures Hal's final rejection of him. It repays close examination.

Both are in an irritable mood early on in the scene. The prince shows this in the Francis encounter. As to the fat knight, he has just suffered the indignity of being robbed of the money he had robbed from others. Not suspecting that the second robbery was by the prince, he is indignant at what he believes merely to be Hal's desertion at the fight. He is bolder and more provocative than usual, and Hal is less forgiving.

Falstaff all but accuses Hal of cowardice – though when directly challenged on the point, declines to make the charge absolute. Nevertheless he delivers the nearest thing he ever comes to a serious insult, telling Hal: 'You are straight enough in the shoulders, you care not who sees your back.' By contrast with his conviction that Hal is a coward, he has by now thoroughly convinced himself that he, Falstaff, is a hero. Though knowing perfectly well that he had hacked his own sword to make it look as if it had been in a fight, and that he had made his nose bleed and smeared the blood over his clothes to support the lie, he nevertheless embarks on a tale of fantastic heroism with all the marks of conviction. By ludicrous multiplication a dozen foes become a hundred. The 'two rogues in buckram' with whom Falstaff fought (i.e. Hal and Poins) become four, then seven, then nine, then eleven, within as many lines of his account; they are then seconded by three more in Kendal green. In his fantasy-combat, Falstaff is almost as imaginative as Hotspur. His imaginative power is immediately pressed into urgent service, since Hal confronts him with the truth and demands how Falstaff can escape it. Falstaff duly obliges with a splendidly inventive lie; that he knew Hal all along, but his loyal instinct forbade him to fight against the heir-apparent.

Falstaff's evident capacity here to play imaginative roles with complete belief is soon called upon again in the little burlesque plays, featuring Hal and himself, with which they apparently seal their reconciliation. It is interesting that Hal has already also limbered up for this occasion by his brief caricature of Hotspur's domestic life, at the end of the Francis episode:

> he that kills me some six of seven dozen of Scots at a breakfast, washes his hands, and says to his wife, 'Fie upon this quiet life. I want work.' 'O my sweet Harry', says she, 'how many hast thou killed today?' 'Give my roan horse a drench', says he, and answers, 'Some fourteen', an hour after.

The caricature is somewhat wide of the mark, but it illustrates that Hal, like Falstaff, is disposed to think in terms of the kind of of fictions which favour himself. When, therefore, the two men engage on their twin plays of king and prince, alternating the two roles, there is perhaps little chance that fiction will favour the objective truth. Instead, it will probably reveal without concealment each man's self-opinion. This turns out to be the case, and these opinions are seen to centre on the vital question of the relationship in which the two men stand to each other.

Falstaff is the first to play the part of reproachful king. Moving from a passable imitation of heroic-play blank verse, and then of Lylyan prose, he rapidly reaches his principal theme: not so much the vices of Hal, but the virtues of one of his companions – 'and yet there is a virtuous man whom I have oft noted in thy company'. . . . 'corpulent; of a cheerful look, a pleasing eye, and a most noble carriage; and, as I think, his age some fifty, or, by'r lady inclining to three-score. And now I remember me, his name is Falstaff.'

Impatiently, however, Hal then seizes the 'throne', reverses the roles, and embarks on a systematic and abrasive rebuttal of the value of Falstaff. Notable among the list of insults are the following charges:

> . . . that reverend Vice, that gray Iniquity, that Father Ruffian, that Vanity in years. . . . That villainous abominable misleader of youth, Falstaff, that old white-bearded Satan.

The accusations of Satanic influence are very prominent here. In effect, Hal, impersonating his father, is making his father blame Hal's vices on his other father, his 'Father Ruffian', Falstaff. Falstaff is the tempter, the abominable misleader of youth. Even the term 'reverend *Vice*' contains a reference to the satanic figure of The Vice who features as tempter in Tudor morality plays.

Critics have not failed to take their cue from these words. The connection with morality drama has been developed to point out that in these plays there is the common theme of prodigal sons and the misleading of youth; that the tempters in such plays commonly masquerade as good tavern-companions; that *Henry IV* frequently mentions the word 'prodigal'; and that

Falstaff, at the end of Part 1, carrying off the body of Hotspur, would remind a contemporary audience of the figure of The Vice, bearing off a soul to Hell.

Whether or not we accept that Shakespeare intended us to recognise Falstaff as Satanic tempter will, of course, crucially affect our reception of his final rejection. If we accept the parallel as intended, then perhaps it makes it easier for us to understand his banishment. Another possible interpretation, however, is to grant that his rejection is required by the play *without* necessarily accepting him to be intended as a tempter. On one theory, by the end of Part 2, Falstaff threatens no small disorder. If as he hopes, 'the laws of England are at my commandment', anarchy would surely ensue. Already, with the arrest of Doll on a charge of murder, Eastcheap looks less harmless than formerly. Yet Falstaff as tempter is another matter. It is noticeable that the accusation is almost wholly Hal's own. It is Hal who casts Falstaff as his tempter. In doing so, he prepares for the final rejection at the end of Part 2. There, once again, he casts Falstaff as 'The tutor and the feeder of my riots', and proceeds to banish him as evidence of his reform: 'I have turned away my former self; / So will I those that kept me company' [2, v iv].

Yet, in his eulogy over what he takes to be the corpse of Falstaff, near the end of Part 1, Hal stresses his own immunity:

> O, I should have a heavy miss of thee
> If I were much in love with vanity.   [1, v iv]

He is fundamentally as unmoved by what Falstaff represents as by the 'proud titles' he has won from Hotspur. He had pacified his father with the promise to collect from Hotspur all the honour he had accrued; when the time to collect actually arrives, he allows Falstaff to be credited with Hotspur's conquest. The impression is very strong of a man with a hidden purpose, who is neither to be deflected, nor to be tempted. If he chooses to place Falstaff in the Satanic role, this is because it better suits the myth of transformation he is preparing for his accession.

It is a myth which operates by contrasts and by display. In the 'I know you all' speech [1, I ii end], Hal produces a whole series of metaphors of brilliance, set off against darkness: the sun against clouds, holidays against work, gold against foil. It is with considerable relish emerging through his 'sadness' that, on his accession, he announces the transformation, and his intention 'To mock the expectation of the world, / To frustrate prophecies, and to raze out / Rotten opinion, who hath writ me down / After my seeming' [2, v ii end]. It is an attitude and an approach to the idea of role-playing and identity which Hal actually shares with his father. In their first interview [1, iii ii], King Henry's speeches emphasise again and again his own cunning as the master of the public performance, and how deficient in the art his son now seemed. He lays precisely the same stress on the value of a precious thing being enhanced artificially; though in his case, his theory stresses the value of rarity. Their major interview in Part 2, at King Henry's death-bed, finds the king still giving the same kind of advice, relating kingship to the whole idea of an artificially-composed display. Even the crusade is confessed to be a political ploy, to direct men's eyes in the right direction: 'I . . . had a purpose now / To lead out many to the Holy Land, / Lest rest and lying still might make them look / Too near unto my state' [2, iv iv]. In both scenes it is by revealing to his father something of 'the noble change [he] has purposèd' that Hal succeeds in comforting the anxious king. This is, however, more than an astute appeal to the kind of argument his father would understand. Both men see kingship as a feat of public relations. They are fundamentally alike.

This is rather ironic, since, when they are together, they clearly fail to understand each other. They play rather stereotyped roles with each other. Henry is a type of the disappointed father, eloquently lamenting the degeneracy of modern times, and the ingratitude and treachery of his son; Hal is the head-hanging penitent. Still more ironically, the immediate cause of dissention in the scene in Part 2 is Hal's removal of the crown from his father's pillow, believing him to be dead. It is a very striking action, indicating Hal's innate appetite for power. The irony is that this appetite is a feature he has inherited from his father. It is, in fact, by promising to guard with his life what his father won that Hal finally wins his father's love back, before he dies.

By this – and by a lie; or rather, by a little fiction:

> Coming to look on you, thinking you dead,
> And dead almost, my liege, to think you were,
> I spake unto this crown as having sense,
> And thus upbraided it: 'The care on thee depending
> Hath fed upon the body of my father;
> Therefore thou best of gold, art worse than gold.
> Other, less fine in carat, is more precious,
> Preserving life in medicine potable;
> But thou, most fine, most honoured most renowned,
> Hast eat thy bearer up.' Thus, my most royal liege,
> Accusing it, I put it on my head,
> To try with it, as with an enemy
> That had before my face murdered my father.   [2, IV iv]

The fiction is attractive; but we saw Hal put the crown on his
head, and he did and said no such thing. The fact is, that he can
only make emotional contact with his father through a fiction,
since role-playing has become his whole identity. So, a little
later, when he enters wearing the crown to meet his brothers, it
is with another image of display that he adopts grief for his
father's death:

> Sorrow so royally in you appears
> That I will deeply put the fashion on
> And wear it in my heart.   [2, v ii 51–3]

Yet, once again, role-playing is ironically another feature Hal
shares with his father. In the battle of Shrewsbury the king
sends out many men to impersonate him; when the Douglas
finally corners the real man, he is mistaken for 'another
counterfeit'. To see King Henry as a 'Player King' would
perhaps explain the sense we often have of the stiltedness of his
speeches.

    It becomes increasingly clear, then, that Falstaff, the 'Father
Ruffian', neither truly influences nor shares characteristics with
Hal. In these two plays, which put considerable stress on the
idea of inherited blood – the word 'blood', in the sense of
lineage, is repeated again and again – the blood Hal inherits is
wholly from his father the king. As part of the display of reform,

Hal does indeed claim that

> The tide of blood in me
> Hath proudly flowed in vanity till now.
> Now doth it turn, and ebb back to the sea,
> Whence it shall mingle with the state of floods,
> And flow henceforth in formal majesty.   [2, v ii 129–33]

The implication here is that formerly his blood was wild; now it is tamed to majesty. Yet all the other references to blood in these plays tend to stress that Hal's blood is, like his father's, rather cold than hot. When King Henry attempts to instruct his other sons how to manage Hal's temper when he comes to kingship, he alleges that, while charitable and tender-hearted, Hal is also irascible. Yet the images Henry uses for Hal's anger are cold, not hot: 'being incensed, he's flint, / As humorous as winter, and as sudden / As flaws congealèd in the spring of day' [2, iv iv 33–5]. The thought is supported even by Hal's other 'father', Falstaff. In the aftermath of Prince John's conquest of the archbishop's rebellion by a dirty trick, Falstaff passes judgement on this brother of Hal, in his famous speech on sack and its virtues. Prince John is despised as cold-blooded, a vice compounded by abstemiousness. Falstaff draws a distinction between John and his elder brother:

> . . . Hereof comes it that Prince Harry is valiant: for the cold blood he did naturally inherit of his father he hath like lean, sterile, and bare land manured, husbanded and tilled, with excellent endeavour of drinking good and good store of fertile sherris, that he is become very hot and valiant. . . .   [2, iv iii 114–20]

As we have already seen, he is wrong in supposing either that Hal is a lover of drink or that drinking has heated his blood. The diagnosis of cold blood, inherited from Henry iv seems, however, accurate enough. The king himself convicts himself of this: 'My blood hath been too cold and temperate, / Unapt to stir at these indignities' [1, i iii 1–2]. As to Hal's inheriting Henry's blood, Henry himself has no doubt of it; he is convinced that God has designed Hal as a scourge for his father's sins: 'out of my blood, / He'll breed revengement and a scourge for me' [1, iii ii 6–7].

With these points in mind it is interesting to return to the mock-reprimand scene [1, II iv], and take a look at the quite different interpretation Falstaff puts on his relationship with Hal in his attempt to rebut the accusation that he is 'a devil' haunting the prince 'in the likeness of a fat old man'. It is an alternative interpretation which is put forward with increasing earnestness as it becomes apparent to Falstaff that he is in effect 'on trial' by a man whom he has taken for no more than a companion, but who here stands in the person of a king.

In their first scene together in Part 1, Falstaff had already given his own amusing version of the temptation motif:

> . . . thou . . . art, indeed, able to corrupt a saint. Thou hast done much harm upon me, Hal, God forgive thee for it. Before I knew thee Hal, I knew nothing, and now am I, if a man should speak truly, little better than one of the wicked. . . .   [I ii 90–4]

In earnest, however, in the later scene, the theory he produces is that his very frailty of flesh is a token of his essential humanity:

> . . . If to be old and merry be a sin, then many an old host that I know is damned: if to be fat is to be hated, then Pharaoh's lean kine are to be loved. No, my good lord! banish Peto, banish Bardolph, banish Poins – but for sweet Jack Falstaff, kind Jack Falstaff, true Jack Falstaff, valiant Jack Falstaff – and therefore more valiant, being as he is old Jack Falstaff – banish not him thy Harry's company, banish not him thy Harry's company. Banish plump Jack, and banish all the world.   [II iv 457–65]

The speech is obviously written to be delivered in frantic haste. By the repetitions, at the end, Falstaff is almost babbling. The essential argument, however, is perfectly coherent. It is a plea that his vices – of eating, drinking and being fat – should be construed as the tokens of essential good nature; that such faults are ineradicable. To try to expunge them would be to contend against life and humanity itself. He returns to his theme later in Part 1, telling Hal, 'thou knowest in the state of innocency Adam fell, and what should poor Jack Falstaff do in the days of villainy? Thou seest I have more flesh than another man, and therefore more frailty' [III iii 162–6]. In the allusion to

Adam, there is again a reference to the Fall, and to the concept that sin can never be escaped by man. In the equation of flesh and frailty there is, apart from an excellent joke, a plea that feasting and drinking should be interpreted as the sign of good spirits. Falstaff is once again pleading, despite his frailty, the essential innocence of his faults.

Certainly, it is true that the plays many times seem to associate Falstaff with feasts and plumpness. Even Hal's insults in the mock-reprimand scene include a description of him as 'that roasted Manningtree ox with the pudding in his belly'. This is what John Dover Wilson calls, 'laying the physical foundations of the Falstaff myth', and its result is to persuade us to think of him in connection with plenty and with festival. We almost always see him in company, very seldom alone; so that he becomes, not a private man, but a kind of public property and the creature of convivial society. This is an impression enhanced by his ability to entertain; and of course he estab-lishes a special link with us, the audience, speaking directly to us, to entertain us with his comic monologues on the themes of honour and sherris-sack. All these impressions dispose us to accept Falstaff's self-apology, 'banish plump Jack, and banish all the world'. It is an apology, however, which is directed, within the play, to an abstemious and unsympathetic judge; one who is unlikely to forgive, as a good joke, little discrepan-cies in Falstaff's account of himself (*valiant* Jack Falstaff, for instance).

Hal's famous reply to the 'banish not' plea is, 'I do, I will'. There is no doubt that Hal is not 'playing'. He is in earnest. The change of tense, from 'I do' to 'I will' is the deliberate signal of a *change* from play to earnest. It is an arresting, an unsettling theatrical moment. The most obvious way of producing it in the theatre is to allow it to stop the show; to stop the actors in their tracks, reduce everything to silence, broken only by the knocking at the door. Falstaff looks at Hal, and realisation dawns that he means what he says.

The most charitable explanation of Hal's words is that they are a warning to an old friend. In the theatre, however, this is not how they sound. It is rather a moment of hostility, consistent with the nagging abrasiveness Hal shows towards Falstaff throughout the scene: the continual reminders of

Gadshill that he insists on making, the references to cowardice, the refusal to let Falstaff 'get away with it'.

In another sense, it is a kind of rehearsal, with Hal shouldering Falstaff aside and seizing the role of king. Falstaff points out that this is a kind of mock-*deposition* – a word which is never neutral in the reign of Henry IV. Hal is both recalling to our mind faint echoes of his father's seizure of the crown, and anticipating his own premature placing of the crown on his own head before his father is dead. But having assumed the role of king, there is certainly no humour in what Hal says. It is a sermon on the themes of grace and temptation, on years and vanity, on surfeit and indecency. His estimate of Falstaff's worth is 'nothing'.

Self-righteousness is perhaps the final characteristic Hal's blood inherits from his father. King Henry always tends to adopt a high moral tone towards rebellion. It is not until his death-scene that he acknowledges any fault in his possession of the crown. His son betrays the same characteristic in the mock-reprimand scene, and, having rehearsed it there, gives us the finished performance at the end of Part 2. There, he returns to his themes of white hairs and indecency, surfeit, age and vanity. This time, however, the rejection is public; and Falstaff, despite his attempts to rally, is broken by the lofty contempt of 'I know thee not, old man. Fall to thy prayers'.

Without doubt, Falstaff must be rejected. The reason why so many audiences have reacted to the rejection with shock and revulsion is because it is public; because Falstaff is being made to feature in a little public drama of the Prodigal Redeemed; because his humiliation is used as a public relations exercise. Perhaps, also, we can never assent to rating Falstaff's value to *us* as 'nothing'. Where the new King Henry V threatens to narrow the sense of values, Falstaff seems to broaden them. But certainly there was no longer room for both men in a single play. Shakespeare's guilty promise in the Epilogue to reintroduce Sir John was never fulfilled.* Instead, in *Henry V*, he killed him off, and gave him a loving eulogy. But then, when the 'Father Ruffian' had attempted to welcome his 'son' – 'God

---

*Not in the context and character recognisable in *Henry IV*, that is. The Falstaff of *The Merry Wives of Windsor* has traits in common with the Falstaff of Eastcheap, Shrewsbury field and Shallow's house, but is a markedly different character-conception.

save thee, my sweet boy' – and had been rejected, Falstaff had perhaps been effectively killed already.

The director of the play has room for manoeuvre here. The speech of rejection departs just sufficiently from its initial high-minded tone, to justify a gentler rejection on stage. Nevertheless, the new king speaks of *despising* his former life. And there is one other point to be made; he speaks of allowing Falstaff liberty and a modest competence of life. Yet, after his exit, Falstaff is arrested and carried off to prison. Are we to interpret the king's apparent mercy merely as a public show? Certainly, any production which wishes to interpret Hal, not as scheming but as impulsive, has a good deal of work to do. As it happens, this is what the most intelligent modern production of the play has set out to do, and its case is highly persuasive and attractive.

PART TWO: PERFORMANCE

6 INTRODUCTION

The following four widely different productions have been
chosen for description and comparison, as contributing most to
our understanding of key themes of *Henry IV*, and of the range of
possibility in the interpretation of character and staging.

1. The RSC production of 1964 at Stratford-upon-Avon,
directed by Peter Hall, John Barton and Clifford Williams;
designed by John Bury and with music by Guy Wolfenden; Eric
Porter as Henry IV, Ian Holm as Hal, Roy Dotrice as Hotspur
and as Justice Shallow, Janet Suzman as Lady Percy, Patience
Collier as Mistress Quickly, Susan Engel as Doll Tearsheet,
Hugh Griffith as Falstaff.

2. The RSC production of 1975 at Stratford-upon-Avon,
directed by Terry Hands; designed by Farrah, lighting by
Stewart Leviton, and with music by Guy Wolfenden; Emrys
James as Henry IV, Alan Howard as Hal, Stuart Wilson as
Hotspur, Ann Hasson as Lady Percy, Maureen Pryor as
Mistress Quickly, Mikel Lambert as Doll Tearsheet, Sydney
Bromley as Justice Shallow, Brewster Mason as Falstaff.

3. The RSC production of 1982 at the Barbican Theatre,
London, directed by Trevor Nunn; designed by John Napier,
lighting by David Hersey, and with music by Guy Wolfenden;
Patrick Stewart as Henry IV, Gerard Murphy as Hal, Timothy
Dalton as Hotspur, Harriet Walter as Lady Percy, Miriam
Karlin as Mistress Quickly, Gemma Jones as Doll Tearsheet,
Robert Eddison as Justice Shallow, Joss Ackland as Falstaff.

4. The BBC TV production, first broadcast in December 1979,
directed by David Giles; designed by Don Homfrey, and with
make-up by Elizabeth Moss; Jon Finch as Henry IV, David
Gwillim as Hal, Tim Piggott-Smith as Hotspur, Michele
Dotrice as Lady Percy, Brenda Bruce as Mistress Quickly,

Frances Cuka as Doll Tearsheet, Robert Eddison as Justice Shallow, Anthony Quayle as Falstaff. (This version has had international release, with repeat showings.)

A word about the choice of productions: with three Royal Shakespeare Company productions and a BBC production, my choice is more 'institutional' than I would have preferred. The reason is simply the absence of suitable alternatives. Since *Henry IV* is in two parts, each a full-length play in its own right, productions of it are comparatively rare – except, that is, by the two institutions committed to making the whole of Shakespeare available. Although there were alternatives, these proved on the whole unilluminating. In the end, I have preferred, whatever the incidental disadvantages, to use a good production rather than a bad one.

7   HENRY AND HAL: 'A FATHER TO MY YOUTH'

The traditional portrayal of Henry IV has been in terms of anguished guilt. John Gielgud's performance in the Orson Welles film *The Chimes at Midnight* (1967) might be called the classic example. Here the king seemed at once ennobled and soured by his burden of conscience. The voice was majestic, but the face betrayed the dyspeptic sufferings of a man for whom life had turned bitter.

'Uneasy lies the head that wears a crown' – Stratford 1964

In the 1964 RSC production (directed jointly by Peter Hall, John Barton and Clifford Williams), Henry was played by Eric Porter. In his interpretation, the king was less bilious than stricken. Dignified – even graceful – in movement and voice, his eyes were haunted by the past. At times, with a characteristic gesture of raising his hands, he seemed to be trying to ward off his ghosts. Even at the beginning there was the aura of the penitential. The stage, in John Bury's design, had massive metal-plated walls as a set; a high-stepped throne; a vast pentangular metal council table; but also, at the back, a narrow stained-glass window. Priests haunted the scene. By Part 2, Henry had assumed a costume of monkish simplicity: a thick coarse robe, tied at the waist with a rope.

Increasingly, the king's energies seemed spent. Doctors were constantly in attendance. At the battle of Shrewsbury he tottered almost helpless under the onslaught of the Douglas. At the end of Part 2, he summed up his victories: how 'everything lies level with our wish'; then, sitting at the edge of his narrow bed, he sighed. There was a long pause before his next words: 'Only we want a little personal strength.'

Yet, in the vital matter of his relationship with Hal there seemed not even the contact of pity between father and son. Their meeting in Part 1 was played with great physical and emotional distance between the two men. When the time came for Hal (Ian Holm) to declare his loyalty, he first went over and closed the door: a telling gesture with its suggestion of guarded secrecy. He remained inaccessible to his father.

'This vile politician, Bolingbroke' – Stratford 1975

Other directors have taken widely differing approaches. The most innovative was certainly Terry Hands's 1975 RSC production at Stratford, with Emrys James cast as Henry.

In this revolutionary interpretation, Henry was presented as being far from inert. This was an abrasive self-made man: contemptuous, possessive, domineering. He was a man who courted aggression. In his first brush with the Northern lords, over the issue of Mortimer's ransom [1, I iii], he followed Hotspur across the stage to stab a blunt finger at his face on 'he never did encounter with Glendower'. Openly laughing at Hotspur, he turned to give Blunt his cue to join in the laugh, which he dutifully did. Returning to the throne, Henry peremptorily beckoned Northumberland across to him, only to dismiss him with another stab of the finger: 'We license your departure with your son.'

A particularly striking detail in this scene – one which reinforced the impression of Henry as a ruthless business-man

– involved the use of a coin. Arguing that Mortimer would have to be ransomed from Wales at the Percy family's own cost, with not 'one penny' of the crown's money spent on rescuing a 'traitor', Henry flung down a coin at Hotspur's feet. Yet as if to reinforce the idea of 'not one penny', he checked his exit at the end of the interview and came back to retrieve the coin from the stage.

With such a man as this, one could well understand the hatred the Percy faction bore him. He was insufferable; his aggression made friendship, even compromise, impossible.

Interestingly, Emrys James's Henry clearly alienated his own son, played by Alan Howard. Here, of course, the king wished to inspire love rather than hate. His affection, however, was just as aggressive as his hatred. He seemed to need to possess Hal: seizing him, dragging him down into his lap, kissing him resoundingly, even on the lips. It was small wonder that Hal recoiled with some revulsion. When, before the battle of Shrewsbury, the prince stepped forward to give defiance to Worcester, his father brusquely pulled him back, and took over.

The reaction of Hal is clearly a vital component of Henry's own uneasiness. As already seen, the king interprets his son's behaviour in terms of a divine punishment for his own misdeeds [1, iii ii]. With the king occupying only a relatively minor portion of the plays which bear his name, the scenes with his son assume a proportionately greater significance.

The problem with the 1975 RSC interpretation of Henry is that the father's unattractiveness explains all too easily the son's antipathy. The question of a punishment for Henry's sins in the past becomes irrelevant in the face of his behaviour in the present. Nevertheless, the 1975 production enjoyed the considerable advantage of signalling very clearly the idea of Hal's 'two fathers'. As Hal recoiled from his natural father, his adopted home was in Eastcheap, with Falstaff. There he seemed completely at ease. This was illustrated in Part 1, iii ii and the following scene.

First, however, it should be explained that Terry Hands's production used a technique of the 'overlapping' of stage-sets. Often, the stage-furniture used for one scene was left on-stage during the next, even though that might be located in a quite different place. And often, even the characters who had appeared in the previous scene would hang about at the end of it and silently look on at the next. So, at the end of II iv – a tavern scene – some barrels and tankards were left on-stage during the first two scenes of Act III. The second scene of the Act is that of Henry's reprimand of his son and, at the end of it, of their reconciliation. As already mentioned, Henry marked his satisfaction over the reconciliation by seizing and kissing Hal. The prince's recoil was exemplified, in Alan Howard's performance, by his breaking free on Blunt's entry, crossing to one of the barrels left on-stage, picking up a tankard by it, and beginning to drink. This very small detail, which does not go unnoticed by the king, is characteristic of Hal's instinctive recoil from the court, and his equally instinctive recourse to the tavern-world as his home and refuge.

Yet undoubtedly the emotional centre of Terry Hands's production was the second reconciliation of father and son, in Part 2. If, in the greater part of the plays, Hal had seemed emotionally regressive – swishing a stick like a small boy, even sucking a thumb, always retreating to Falstaff for comfort – the second reconciliation scene [IV iv] marked his growing-up.

Given the aggressiveness with which Emrys James played the king, the scene predictably started in near-hysteria. Awaking to find the crown gone (removed by Hal), Henry rose from his bed of terminal illness to jump on a chair and rant at his son. Snatching the crown, he rammed it back on Hal's head; falling to his knees, he crawled around the bed before collapsing on to it. His prophecy of the ruin of his kingdom was a howl of pain. Yet the audience had already seen from Alan Howard's performance that this was a different Hal. When he first placed the crown on his own head, his face registered anguish as well as wonderment. He blinked as if subjected to a blinding light, but immediately his voice seemed to take on a new authority. When therefore he realised his father was still alive, and that he had robbed him of his crown, he reacted with a quite new moral sensibility. When the king jammed the crown back on his head, Hal cried out in protest. His self-abasement in making his apology was painful to watch, and the reconciliation of father and son intensely moving.

For the remainder of the scene, Hal acted almost as the

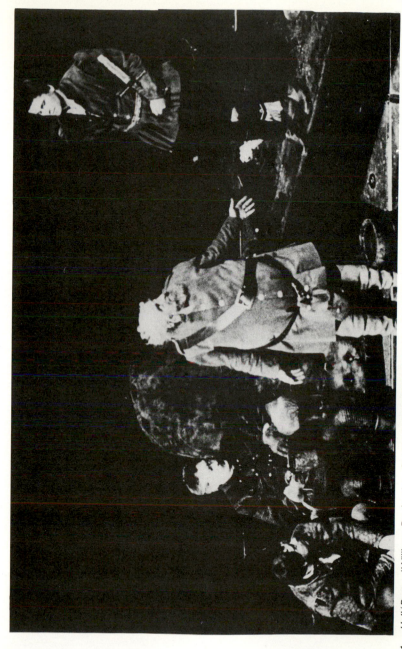

1. *Hall/Barton/Williams Production, Stratford, 1964.* Prince Hal (Ian Holm) and Falstaff (Hugh Griffith): 'I do, I will' (Part 1, Act II, sc. iv) Poins (Clive Swift), Bardolph (John Normington). Photograph: courtesy of the Governors of the Royal Shakespeare Theatre, Stratford-upon-Avon.

2. *Hall/Barton/Williams Production, Stratford, 1964.* Hotspur (Roy Dotrice): 'Let each man do his best' (Part 1, Act V, sc. ii). Photograph courtesy of the Governors of the Royal Shakespeare Theatre, Stratford-upon-Avon.

3. *Terry Hands Production, Stratford, 1975.* Hal/Henry V (Alan Howard), Falstaff (Brewster Mason): 'God save thee, my sweet boy!' (Part 2, Act V, sc. v). Photograph © Joe Cocks.

4. *David Giles's BBC TV Production, 1979.* Prince Hal (David Gwillim): 'Lo, here it sits' (Part 2, Act IV, sc. iv). BBC copyright photograph.

5. *Trevor Nunn's Production, Barbican, 1982.* Henry IV (Patrick Stewart) and Prince Hal (Gerard Murphy). The second reprimand/reconciliation scene (Part 2, Act IV, sc. v). Photograph © Donald Cooper.

6. *Trevor Nunn's Production, Barbican, 1982.* Hal/Henry V (Gerard Murphy), Falstaff (Joss Ackland). 'Presume not that I am the thing I was' (Part 2, Act V, sc. v). Photograph © Donald Cooper.

attentive nurse of his father: supporting him, making him comfortable, retrieving the crown and giving it to him – and finally carrying him out in his arms. The lines at the end of the scene (where other characters should enter) were cut in this production so that this highly emotional reunion should be undiluted.

'His temper therefore must be well observed' – Barbican 1982

Another production making good use of Hal's youth in interpreting his character is that of Trevor Nunn in 1982 at the Barbican Theatre, London. Perhaps even more than the RSC's 1975 production at Stratford, this one performed by the same national company sought to explain Hal's truancy in terms of adolescent rebellion.

In the 1982 production, however, the impulse seemed to come very much from Hal himself, as played by Gerard Murphy. There was much less obvious reason for his behaviour, largely because the king was far less obviously obnoxious as a man.

In fact, in Patrick Stewart's interpretation of the role, the king emerged almost as a nobody. Neither as sick as Eric Porter's Henry IV nor as aggressive as Emrys James's, he is a man in whom almost everything is clamped down under control and neutralised. His costume is the plainest imaginable: a simple white tunic, buttoned high at the neck; black trousers, just visible, tucked into black knee-boots. This was the costume – reminiscent of a Russian kulak – which was revealed beneath his golden cloak of office in the first scene of Part 1; and he wore it throughout, except during the battle. It indicated cleanliness and fastidiousness – an impression reinforced by his short-cut hair, his extreme economy of movement, and the characteristic habit of taking a refined sip of cordial from a goblet that was always at hand for him when he entered and sat.

During the quarrel scene with the Percy leaders [1, i iii], all the men at the council table were won over by Hotspur's impulsive speech of excuse for the refusal to yield his prisoners' ransoms – all save the king. At one point, as Hotspur bent down at Henry's side, 'beseeching' his tolerance, he leaned his arm on the table. Henry moved his hand forward. For an instant, as the hand hesitated, it seemed as if he was going to lay it on Hotspur's arm. But he then reached past him for his goblet, and the moment – and the opportunity for peace that it offered – was gone for ever.

In the first reconciliation scene with Hal [1, III ii], the same tightly inhibited Henry was evident. There was the same almost prim fastidiousness about the set. The king sat in a sparsely furnished room, with only a table, a chair and a ewer for washing his hands. The table and the ewer-stand were covered with purple cloths, each with a small gold emblem of the crown. Henry kept his son standing. He yielded nothing. Rather, he actually produced, from a drawer in the table, the bags which had been stolen at Gadshill, slamming them down on the table. Crossing to Hal and carrying a cushion, he perched it on his son's head, making him both feel and look a fool, wearing his mock-crown as he had done in the earlier tavern-scene. Returning to his seat, as Hal began his apology in earnest, the king hardly looked at him. He wore, in fact, his most characteristic facial expression: eyes screwed up tight, mouth twisted into an ambiguous ironic smile. Only at the very end of the prince's speech did Henry's expression seem less sardonic, and the son was permitted, for a few seconds, an expression of genuine pleasure on 'A hundred thousand rebels die in this'. Then, immediately, he tidied the bags back into the drawer of his table and bent back to his paper-work, hardly raising his eyes to his son again. The pattern was repeated again and again. The tight quiet manner very occasionally broke down – as when Henry shouted at his son or at Worcester – to betray the force of feeling inside the man. But whenever a genuine impulse seemed about to escape, he choked it back. When Worcester came to present the dissidents' grievances and Hal made his offer of single combat against Hotspur [1, v i], the idea seemed momentarily to seize the king's imagination. Patrick Stewart almost ran down from his balcony position to the main stage. On the instant he reached it, however, he checked. The sober control returned, and Henry's next words came out almost stiffly: 'Albeit considerations infinite / Do make against it.'

In Part 2, Henry became even less expressive. The 'book of fate' speech [III i] seemed deliberately underplayed. When his collapse finally came [IV iv], he was laid to rest on a bed (tilted forward in a wedge-shape, for visibility), where he lingered for the remainder of his 'life'. His by-now customary demeanour of a man suffering absurd injuries was merely a little heightened in the second crisis with his son. Warwick's disclosure that Hal had been found in tears over the 'stolen' crown was received with a harsh laugh. The king's recriminations to his son were delivered with violent sarcasm. Throughout Hal's long apology, Henry twisted his face away, his true reaction veiled in a sardonic grimace of a smile. It was not clear until his loud cry 'O my son', and his embrace of Hal, how he was responding. Then all his remaining energies were summoned to rattle out his last desperate advice to his successor: a political homily to which Hal, thinking more of his father's death than of his own succession, seemed hardly to hear.

When told that his death-chamber was called 'Jerusalem', Henry alone saw the bitter joke of having been assured that he would die in Jerusalem, and of having thought it meant the Holy Land. Altogether, in Part 2, King Henry in Trevor Nunn's production became a figure who realised the sour jest that life had played on him and his ambitions. He became a man obsessively working himself to death with papers and state-business, knowing that everything he did was pointless.

It was to this man that his son finally responded. For the bulk of the two plays, Gerard Murphy's Hal had been a young man whose feelings and responses to most other men had been confused and contradictory. Suddenly, everything became simple. He responded to his father's imminent death with a complete abandonment to grief: his nose blocked and his voice choked with tears, knuckles in his eyes, his whole body shaking with sobs. Since Gerard Murphy was a stocky well-built Hal, this came over with great theatrical force. The prince who had suffered from such an uncertain and fluctuating temper, who had been such a creature of moods, had finally discovered in himself an uncomplicated and unsullied emotion. He had suddenly found that he had loved his father.

As with Terry Hands's production at Stratford in 1975, this of Trevor Nunn at the Barbican in 1982 was again an interpretation of 'growing up'. Earlier in the performance, Hal had seemed a particularly loutish, awkward youth. He had so often moved or stood awkwardly, his face contorted into improbable grimaces, violently shaking his head and his shock of fair hair. Hereafter, all these gauche mannerisms were gone. His father's death had taught him how to be a man.

'How came I by the crown, O God forgive' – Television 1979

In all three of the interpretations we have been discussing, one common factor is detectable in regard to the relationship of father and son, among widely differing emphases. It is that, however Hal responds to his father, the king emerges as a figure who is tightly bound up in his own obsessions. He need not be exactly withdrawn. Emrys James's extrovert King Henry in Terry Hands's production shows this. Yet he gives very little to his son. If understanding can be achieved between them, it falls to Hal to penetrate the barriers, not only in himself, but also in his father.

In this respect, the production of the *Henry IV* plays in the BBC's televised 'complete Shakespeare' series ran entirely true to form. Directed by David Giles and first broadcast in December 1979, it presented the king, again, as a figure of harsh remoteness. In the end, whatever contact was established between him and his son was made to seem both odd and unsatisfactory.

From the beginning of Part 1, Jon Finch as Henry adopted a highly stylised and stagey delivery of his lines. The words were chanted out, mostly in pedantic monotone. The technique was at its most idiosyncratic in the first reconciliation scene [1, III ii], with the words perversely chopped up into separate syllables ('pro-phet-ic-all-y'), and the lines dessicated into a sing-song iambic 'tune' ('Ŏf év-rў béard-lĕss váin cŏm-párătĭve'). Only the occasional soar in register broke the pattern.

But then, the director had evidently intended that this scene between father and son should be played very 'dead'. Jon Finch delivered his complaints moving forward to the camera to ¾-shot, leaving David Gwillim's Hal in long-shot behind him. Hal watched his father with a face absolutely neutral and lifeless. Whenever his father turned to look at him, Hal looked down, avoiding his eyes, raising his own again only when his father had turned away. He seemed locked in a kind of numbness, until stirred by the king's wilder allegations (that Hal was as much his father's enemy as Hotspur) into self-defence. Yet even here, the scene avoided any sense of real contact. Hal's promises of reform were delivered with a smug half-smile, conveying a sense of secrecy and private knowledge. He remained as immobile as before, giving nothing to his father.

In the corresponding scene in Part 2 [iv iv], the camera was located beyond the king's bed, catching Hal's approach, and behind him, through an open doorway, the nobles of the court watching him. Hal's reaction to what seemed to be his father's death was carefully registered, and the grief seemed strong. Yet, as he bent over to kiss his father, he was stopped by sight of the crown on the pillow. The crown seemed to inspire the greater emotion. He lifted it reverently, wonderingly, up to his own head, his voice trembling with feeling. The kiss for his father was forgotten. (See Plate 4.)

Similarly, when the king then awoke to find the crown gone, its loss revealed tremendous energy still in him, carrying over into his reproaches on Hal's return. Jon Finch was by turns plaintive, bitter, angry, mocking and hysterical in his well-shaped long speech. In the reconciliation it was again the crown which played a central part in the emotions evoked and experienced. David Giles's production stressed strongly that what pacified the king was Hal's little charade of how, thinking his father was indeed dead, he had taken the crown to reproach it. David Gwillim played the charade in an extremely broad and stylised way; and as he established the imaginary relationship with the crown, the camera registered the incredulity on the king's face giving way to tentative belief. Finally, the two men crouched at the foot of the sick-bed as Henry gave his dying advice. Again, it was the crown which seemed to draw the scene's emotions to itself. It was placed prominently between them on the bed; and the final camera shot, before the two men were rejoined by others, was of the king, full-face, pushing the crown across to his son on 'How came I by the crown, O God forgive, / And grant it may with thee in true peace live!'

Using the resources of the camera, to zoom and pan and
track, and home-in on the *visual* focus of a scene, the director
had given the crown a physical centrality impossible on a large
stage. The effect was to establish in our minds the distortion of
emotion in Hal and Henry. There were emotions, but they were
passed from one to the other only through the crown and its
magnetic power to attract avid feeling. Consequently, there
was no final understanding between father and son: only a
shared obsession.

8   THE STATE: 'MY POOR KINGDOM, SICK WITH CIVIL BLOWS'

'I hear the king my father is sore sick' – Comparisons

Of the four productions in discussion, it has been the 1979
television version which has been most explicit about the king's
sickness. There was no genteel enfeeblement here. The king
had a disease. Its symptoms were obvious and distasteful,
copied carefully by Elizabeth Moss in her make-up scheme
from illustrations in a medical book. In Part 2, Jon Finch's face
was progressively invaded by a scarlet and yellow crust around
his mouth, nose and cheeks. His hands were covered with suede
gloves, but both the gloves and the sleeves of his expensive robe
were suggestively discoloured, as if the disease was seeping
through them. Once again, the medium of television was able
economically to draw attention to a central symbol of the play,
by its capacity to close in on detail. In the echoing state-
chamber in which King Henry complained to his other sons
about the sins of his heir, he sat hunched, in his chair, as if cold.
Then he struggled up and stood slightly swaying and percept-
ibly shaking, wringing his gloved hands. The camera 'saw' him
as if peeping through the semi-circle of noblemen around him,
and caught them slightly edging away, glancing nervously at
each other.

The other productions tended to be far less vivid here. In
1964, Eric Porter's Henry had been physically weak from the

start. In his first interview with Hal he had needed smelling-salts, but his disease was evidently slow-moving. By Part 2 he was hollow-eyed, and seemed to have trouble with his breathing, but was nevertheless still mobile. In the 1982 production we had for the most part a king who seemed hardly sick at all. A little tired, perhaps; but until his discreet neat cough into his handkerchief in Part 2 [IV iv], he hardly seemed a dying man. Even then, it was something of a surprise when, rising from his chair and crossing the stage – making a little joke about good news making him ill, as if to pretend that there was nothing the matter – he then fell and started choking. Then, instantly, he seemed close to death, lying in a coma in his bed. One cleverly observed detail worth mentioning is that, when Hal came in and was left with his father, and began to speak about his father's final 'sleep', the king lifted a hand from his bed, faintly beckoning. Hal, however, did not see it.

With the 1975 production, too, illness was something which arrived very late. This was largely due to Terry Hands's overall decision to present the king as a powerful and domineering figure. Everything emphasised this. His costumes had been heavy and opulent. In peace, thick fur robes, and a kind of long scarf, reaching almost from floor to floor, made like woven reeds, but of gold; in war, red and gold, the royal emblems on his breastplate carved out of the metal in massive relief. Only at the scene of Henry's collapse did Emrys James make him appear physically less dominating or even more simply dressed. Then, however, as he spoke of dying and going to lie with his ancestors, he moved down-stage in a kind of eerie corridor of light, looking for the first time vulnerable and pale.

'We are all diseas'd' – *Comparisons*

If, however, the king's disease tended in at least two of these productions to be understated and slow to develop, all four managed to suggest sickness to be more than a matter of one man's physical condition. The 1982 production in particular contrived to suggest that a whole range of minor figures suffered from the general malaise; with Northumberland, especially, played as genuinely infirm, rather than 'crafty-sick', and the Gloucestershire recruits looking a particularly pitiful crew. Most Doll Tearsheets and Bardolphs are played so as to emphasise their peculiar self-inflicted diseases. Here, the 1982 Bardolph (John Rogan) was small, thin, stooped, rheumatic, balding, with sores on his face and arms (but preposterously wearing the kind of broad-striped hose which might have been fashionable when be bought them twenty years previously). One remembers, too, the 1964 Bardolph (John Normington), with his Cyrano-like nose, heavily rutted and encrusted beneath his bristling eyebrows and erratically-sprouting hair; or the 1975 Doll (Mikel Lambert), voluptuously diseased.

The most important factor, however, in suggesting a whole kingdom suffering from degeneracy, is the stage-sets, which establish the whole atmosphere of a production.

Here, the outstanding example is Terry Hands's 1975 production. The designer, Farrah, used a completely bare stage. In the middle was a large tilted ramp. The colour was grey. One reviewer at the time remarked that the stage had been made to look as gaunt as the flight-deck of an aircraft-carrier. Shallow curtains were flown in diagonally across the back of the ramp, to establish location: a red curtain with a boar's head emblem on it for the tavern in Eastcheap; a black curtain for the king's death. Carpets were similarly used. Occasionally, a cart or a huge cross might be brought on, but many scenes were staged without any stage-furniture, and such chairs and tables as were used in the court scenes looked scarcely less artisan than the tavern pieces; indeed the same furniture could be made to do double service. The rebels in Part 1 used their own camp-equipment. Made of leather and thick crossed wooden poles, it was all easily folded for portability. Altogether, the stage remained immensely flexible and unimpeded, with very rapid scene changes possible. Yet the overriding impression, enhanced by Stewart Leviton's pronounced lighting technique of bright white light, or near-darkness, was of a stark gaunt world.

The most striking contribution to this effect came in Part 2. Here, in Farrah's set, a large tangle of heavy branches had been added above the ramp, like a kind of mid-air bridge. Largely because of the lighting trained on these branches, they seemed white and wintry by the end of the play. The stage was strewn with unswept dead leaves (amusingly echoed in Falstaff's battle-camouflage, whereby he had covered himself with foliage). Up-stage lay a cannon, disused and heavily chained, but with a mass of papers stuck to the floor in a pattern as if they had been shot from the cannon's mouth – a rather obvious symbol for the 'Rumour' of Part 2, and for the largely 'paper war' which is waged in the second part. In the Gloucestershire scenes, bird-song lightened the atmosphere. At the end of the play, however, Falstaff stood alone under the bare branches to the sound of the raven's croak. Not surprisingly, then, the prevailing background atmosphere of this 1975 production was sombre.

To a lesser extent this has been true of the other two stage-productions. With the 1964 version (designed by John Bury), the steel-walled set used for the council-chamber scenes would not alone have given this impression. The twin walls of this set were, however, designed so as to rotate. In effect, each steel wall was merely the visible side of a triangle. When the triangles rotated, quite different walls were disclosed. The huge triangles could also be hinged forward or back. The second sides of the triangles disclosed the interior of a tavern, with an open staircase up the side of one wall and a curtained opening in the other. These walls were wooden, but the wood looked blackened, charred and grimy. The tavern furniture was battered and stained. In Part 2, for the Gaultree Forest scenes, the walls hinged right back to disclose three huge 'trees' centre stage, with a dark tangle of branches above and behind them. At Gadshill, in Part 1, the same 'trees' had been gibbets, with a corpse dangling from each.

The 1982 set (designed by John Napier) consisted of four tall wooden structures, each built like the open-section interior of a three-storey square house. Arranged initially in a receding rightangled 'v', each structure could be moved separately backwards or forwards, to build a different 'house' for each location. Often, the structures were full of people, even as they were moved into place, particularly with the tavern-scenes, which became momentarily large portable pubs. At times, the scene practically seethed with extras, working hoists, trundling kegs, mounting ladders to paint signs, bustling about with sacks or trays of drinks, beating carpets, making beds. Yet the

overall impression of these sets remained drab. The boards
were twisted. They were hung with shields and lances, but all
painted black – the colour of the wood itself – and the dark
heavy structures seemed gloomy and overpowering. The effect
was enhanced by David Hersey's lighting: often a dim suffused
light; at other times a bright overhead spotlight, leaving dingy
shadows all around. In addition, Eastcheap extras often
remained on the set, lounging up stairs, watching, during the
intervening court scenes. The effect was to suggest a political
world which was haunted by shabbiness.

'The law of nature' – Comparisons

The final contributing factor in creating a sense of national
malaise is the emphasis placed by some of the productions on
the predatoriness of the world of both politics and private life.

In the 1979 television production, there was the soliloquy by
Falstaff, in Part 2, at the end of Act III. His subject was the
preposterous falsehoods of Justice Shallow. Falstaff gave his
own version of Shallow's 'wild' youth. The camera held the
whole speech as a close-up on Falstaff's face. As he concluded
that, with an old fraud like Shallow so unnaturally elevated to
'beeves' and authority, he, Sir John Falstaff, was entitled by the
law of nature to relieve him of some of his superfluous wealth,
Anthony Quayle's helmeted face (suffused with a ruddy glow of
sunset and alcohol) took on a crafty leering expression. He
ended his line – 'if the young dace be a bait for the old pike, I see
no reason in the law of nature but I may snap at him' – with a
sharp clap of his jaws.

In the 1975 RSC version, two other scenes caught the eye.
When, in Part 2, Falstaff was arrested for debt, at the suit of
Mistress Quickly, by the two beadles, Fang and Snare, these
two officers lived up to their names. One hung on to a leg, the
other leaped on Falstaff's back and gnawed at his neck. In the
later Gaultree Forest sequence – in which the archbishop and
his associates were tricked into surrender and then consigned to
execution – the rebel leaders were surrounded, when the news
of the dispersal of their troops was announced, by a menacing

band of soldiers with spears, closing in on them as if at a boar-hunt.

But every production has contributed its own details to this theme. The point is that all make the same general observation of the savagery of Henry IV's kingdom, however vivid and hilarious a street-life it sustains. Together with the persistent imagery of sickness, and the sombreness of the settings, the production-emphasis has always seemed to be predominantly dark. However bright the intervening episodes, this has always been the framing impression.

9   Falstaff: 'That Old White-Bearded Satan'

It would be true to say that there are two main categories of Falstaff in performances of the *Henry IV* plays. The first Falstaff is the boisterous merry-maker, the convivial sack-guzzler, the lovable reprobate. There may be complications in this kind of portrayal, but the character is still essentially the simple Falstaff of tavern legend.

The second Falstaff is by his nature a more complex creature. Here, the companionable round man becomes an endearing, but never quite convincing, façade – strapped on as a disguise for a man who lives by much more complicated impulses than appetite alone.

On this major division of interpretation, the four productions under consideration break equally into the two camps. Into the second fall the 1979 television production and the 1982 stage version. The 1975 and 1964 stage versions come into the first.

'That huge bombard of sack' – Stratford 1964

The RSC's 1964 production saw a performance of Falstaff which many still consider to be definitive, and which will certainly never be forgotten by those fortunate enough to see it. The performance was by Hugh Griffith, fresh from his film triumph as Squire Western in *Tom Jones*. Precisely the qualities which had made his success in that film now suited him to the part of Falstaff. There was the large physical presence, the roaring, braying, gargling voice with its great sensual range. Perhaps most important, there were the characteristic glittering eyes which, with his sharp features, gave his head a curious eagle-like appearance, atop the enormous body. It was a noisy performance, and far from word-perfect; but it swept the play along with an unstoppable gusto.

Its major complication was the unexpected elegiac quality which Griffith achieved in Part 2. Here the great Tavern scene [II iv] especially evoked this side of Falstaff. After the expulsion of Pistol, Falstaff sat in the gargantuan tub-chair which was his tavern-throne, Doll Tearsheet (played by Susan Engel) on his knee. John Bury's set was packed with domestic detail: a brazier-fire, a large wicker hamper, a clothes-horse draped with the day's washing. Down-stage, the Hostess and Bardolph dozed over their beer. Up-stage, the musicians, squatting on the stairs, played their melancholy tune on recorders. Doll's head lay on Falstaff's shoulder, and she spoke of patching up his old body for heaven. For a long time, Falstaff gazed into the fire, in the smoky dimly-lit room. Then his words, 'Peace, good Doll, do not speak like a death's head; do not bid me remember mine end', had an infinite sadness. His abuse of Hal and Poins was full of a sense of loss: of the youth they still had, but which he had long ago left behind.

This strong sense of pathos was the major note of Part 2 of the production. In the Gloucestershire scenes, the triangular walls of John Bury's set revolved to disclose the half-timbered fascia of Justice Shallow's home, painted saffron yellow and covered with climbing flowers. Between the two walls was a five-barred gate. In front of the house sat Shallow and Silence, sorting the season's bumper crop of apples into barrels from a heaped wheelbarrow. This lovingly-rendered set was inhabited with performances of the fullest human detail. Roy Dotrice's performance as Shallow was a masterpiece.* His frail wispy bespectacled justice was an utterly believable eccentric. Fussy, high-voiced, nimble but tottering, he suddenly acquired mar-

---

*He doubled it with Hotspur, in Part 1. See section 10, below.

vellous comic energy as he remembered and re-enacted how the
'little quiver fellow' managed his caliver at Mile-End Green,
fifty years before; and then had to be helped, breathless back to
his seat. His simple glowing nostalgia was carefully played
against Falstaff's dread of anything that reminded him of the
passing years, and his attempts – 'no more of that' – to suppress
the past.

Nevertheless, Griffith gave basically a simple interpretation
of the part of the fat knight. Gleeful, tender, crafty, baleful by
turns, it created the image of a man with a huge appetite for life,
and an equal dread of losing it. This was exactly what the 1964
production required, with its strong intended contrast between
the life-loving characters (Falstaff, Hotspur, Shallow) and the
emotionally dead world of politics and politicians.

'Sir John with all Europe' – Stratford 1975

Brewster Mason's Falstaff, in the RSC/Hands production of
1975, was essentially a gentleman. Again, what dictated the
casting was an intended contrast; this time specifically with
King Henry. Where Emrys James played Henry as a self-made
man, it was the old knight, ironically, who was majestic. Where
Henry was rasping, Falstaff was benevolent. Where Henry was
deadly serious, Falstaff radiated a sense of fun. From the start,
there was a stress on his harmlessness, and on his easy intimacy
with Hal (Alan Howard). Their relationship was a detailed
study in mild horseplay. The word was almost cued to us on
their first appearance in Part 1, for Falstaff lay under a huge
horse-blanket, in a down-stage corner, Hal beside him, through
the first scene; and was woken by the prince pulling back the
blanket and imitating the sound of a mosquito buzzing in his
ear. When he woke, Hal poured him a drink in his double-
handled quart pot. The Gadshill episode and its aftermath
emerged as a shared joke. When Falstaff came up with his
preposterous excuse for cowardice ('I knew ye'), he emerged
from his chair almost helpless with laughter, taking mock stabs
at Hal with his sword; with Hal staggering backwards and
literally doubling up over a barrel of sack.

Even in Part 2, the Falstaff we saw was a grand old man,

benevolently presiding over his ruffianly 'family', of which Hal still seemed capable of being a boyish and willing member. Only at one or two key points did Falstaff feel the rougher edge of Hal. For the rest of the time, he was simply too jovial, too convivially mellow, too nice a man to respond to with anything but liking. How could one *fail* to like someone who reacted with such mild irritation, and such basic tolerance, to even the picking of his pockets? It was a performance refreshingly innocent of pathos. There was no spiritual dimension whatever to this Falstaff's life. He tried at one point to make the sign of the cross, but found he had forgotten how. He re-learned the trick only by imitating the Lord Chief Justice in Part 2.

'Quick, forgetive, full of nimble, fiery, and delectable shapes' – Television 1979

The 1979 television Falstaff was played by Anthony Quayle. An actor of international status, Quayle had played the part at Stratford-upon-Avon as long ago as 1951. He now played the part with authority. Like the Brewster Mason version of 1975, this Falstaff was a gentleman. At times, when he tilted back his head, raised his eyebrows and pursed his lips, he might almost be described as genteel. His accent certainly matched that word. Yet the performance was also in every way expansive. He seemed to fill all the available space of the small screen, not only physically but vocally – the lines themselves being given a sonorous orchestration of snorts, growls, snuffles and hisses of breath. His extremely flexible vocal range was matched by his mobility of features. His eyes, sometimes so tightly wreathed in creases as to be hardly visible, could bolt open to reveal an astonishing quantity of white. For all his physical immobility, he seemed both sprightly and agile in his gestures. His ruddy face and russet costume brought warmth into any scene he entered.

Yet Anthony Quayle's performance was also of considerable subtlety. Its essential central element was Falstaff's status as a witty performer. Seen in this way, his good spirits and his energy emerged as an act of will, a created role. Falstaff as entertainer was a man who lived by his wits. Correspondingly, he was subject to all the anxieties of his trade. He was a man dependent on his audience, and forever having to trick them and to win their response.

The first time this role was evident was in the major tavern-scene in Part 1 [II iv]. With his lies about Gadshill exposed, he seemed to make a deliberate effort to turn the joke away from himself, and to lead new revels: 'Hostess, clap to the doors – . . . Gallants, lads, hearts of gold, all the titles of good fellowship come to you! What, shall we be merry? Shall we have a play extempore?' Word spread quickly, and by the time the subject of the play was fixed, the room was rapidly filling with extras, eager for entertainment. Falstaff duly turned in a comedian's performance. The lines, funny enough even on the page, were shaped by Quayle into broadly-signposted, cleverly-worked cues for laughter. When, as King Henry, he described the prince's one 'virtuous' companion ('a goodly portly man, i'faith, and a corpulent; of a cheerful look, a pleasing eye, and a most noble carriage'), he then drolly 'threw away' the next line with the definite air of a man providing the laugh his audience was looking for: 'and, as I think, his age some – – fifty?' It was typical of a comic performance that was a kind of collaboration with his audience that he then, with an airy wave of the hand, and a look of querying expectation, made the audience supply the end of the next sentence: 'and now I remember me, his name is – – ' 'FALSTAFF!'.

The same kind of performer was evident in his handling of the Lord Chief Justice in Part 2 [II i]. Here the comedy came from one-line gags, with the Lord Chief Justice (Ralph Michael) being constantly and unwittingly lured into providing the feed-lines. Again, a large audience gathered to hear the fun. Falstaff began by playing to them, constantly turning to them to cue the laughter. By the end, however, the Lord Chief Justice has also been drawn into the performance. His smile was only barely suppressed. His whole manner indicated his pleased awareness at being stooge and collaborator in a comedian's matinee.

Yet Quayle's own performance was at its best in suggesting those moments when *Falstaff's* performance was at its least commanding. Television, of course, permits great subtlety of expression, and the camera could therefore catch the moments of anxiety. At the beginning of the same tavern scene just mentioned, Falstaff was cornered in his seat by Hal and Poins (David Gwillim and Jack Galloway), who stood above and beside him, their faces inches from his. He had become their quarry. With the camera close in on the three faces, and catching moments of panic in Falstaff's as his bluffs were exposed, there was a dreadful blankness in the silence which followed Hal's challenge, 'What trick, what device, what starting-hole canst thou now find out, to hide thee from this open and apparent shame?' For one horrendous moment, Falstaff had no ideas at all. Then, a crafty expression spread over his face, and with a growing guffaw, Falstaff discovered a trick that would serve: 'By the Lord, I knew ye as well as he that made ye.' Panting with comic relief he went on, 'was it for me to kill the heir apparent?'

Undoubtedly, persecution brought out the best in this Falstaff. With no opponent to sharpen his wits, he seemed stupid and fuddled with Doll in Part 2. Set going by an antagonist, he launched into great inventiveness; and, as a typical performer, half-believed his own inventions. His lies about Gadshill, for instance, became for him a re-enactment of his true heroism rather than an invention. He demonstrated his thrusts and parries in all earnestness. Yet, living as he did by fiction, his whole life was invention, and only as successful as his last performance. Always there was the flicker of anxiety between the joke and the laugh. When his audience turned against him, with Hal's final rejection, there was nothing left. He collapsed and shrivelled as if he had been physically deflated. This television Falstaff was an interpretation of great sophistication.

'And now has he land and beeves' – Barbican 1982

Joss Ackland was the Falstaff in the RSC/Nunn production of 1982. He gave us a man who was notably angrier than any other version of the part we have discussed. Full credit was given to Falstaff's undoubted capacity for envy: of Hal's youth, of Hotspur's 'honour', of the 'land and beeves' of Shallow. This

Falstaff was consequently a touchy man, resentful of others and ever-watchful for real or imagined slights.

He was raised to a high pitch of indignation at the beginning of Part 2. Here he emerged in a slightly changed costume from his customary leather jerkin and boots; he now wore epaulettes over the jerkin, with the royal devices of lions and fleurs-de-lys in scarlet, blue and gold. He continued to wear them for almost the whole of Part 2. These were his badges of office, the ostentatious sign of a 'distinguished' war-career. And yet, at the beginning of the play, he fumed with indignation at the tailor who had refused to give credit to him, a war-hero. What strongly emerged here was Falstaff's deeply felt resentment at the disdain he received at the hands of 'respectable' people, especially those who wear 'high shoes and bunches of keys at their girdles'.

This very noticeably spilled over into his brush [2, ıı i] with the Lord Chief Justice (played by Griffith Jones, who had also taken the part in the 1975 production). Falstaff was very little inclined to respond humbly to the judge's clear threat of punishment for the Gadshill robbery. On the line 'I am poor as Job, my lord, but not so patient', he went right up to his antagonist and shouted the words in his face. As with the 1979 television production of this street-scene, Falstaff had gathered a large stage-audience; but here, in Nunn's production, they remained very quiet, looking at each other as if scandalised. Falstaff was definitely daring the Lord Chief Justice, challenging him to do his worst. By now he felt confident of his immunity, after his good-fortune at the battle of Shrewsbury. Joss Ackland gave his frequent mentions of the battle a particularly proud emphasis. Of course, the aggressiveness then wore off into humour. When he was duly rewarded with laughter, he began to show off, swaggering across the stage when preposterously complaining about 'these costermongers' times', and putting on skittish airs when claiming to be in the 'vaward of . . . youth'. When, however, this provoked the Lord Chief Justice's scorn and the boast that he had separated Falstaff from the prince, Falstaff again grew belligerent, jerking his stick in the old man's face, and shouting 'Yea; I thank your pretty sweet wit for it'.

He was as capable of taking offence at Hal. In the Part 1

scene [III iii] which featured the inquisition on the question of who picked Falstaff's pockets, he sat heavily and moodily in his chair throughout. He tried very evidently to pick on Bardolph and the Hostess in turn. When Gerard Murphy's smiling Hal entered, Falstaff refused to respond to him; and Joss Ackland gave special emphasis to some lines which usually pass unnoticed: 'Well, God be thanked for these rebels, they offend none but the virtuous. I laud them, I praise them.' Clearly Falstaff hated the virtuous, and felt that Hal was behaving like one of them. He was deliberately trying to give offence by praising the enemies of Hal's father. He succeeded. When, a little later, Hal began to speak of the need for prompt military action – 'The land is burning, Percy stands on high, / And either they or we must lower lie' – Falstaff responded to this show of zeal and political virtue with fury. The line, 'Rare words! brave world!' were snarled at the prince. 'Hostess, my breakfast, come', was a deliberate cold-shouldering of Hal's war-fever.

This stress of Falstaff's irascibility made him, if anything, actually more effective as a comedian. Where Anthony Quayle in the TV version had conveyed the sense of anxiety in Falstaff himself, this 1982 production stressed the anxiety other people felt about Falstaff. He was a man of uncertain temper, who could turn nasty. When, therefore, he relaxed and performed, his stage audience were evidently relieved. A dozen willing hands heaved him up onto the table for the mock-reprimand scene [1, II iv] and greated his performance with shouts and whistles of pleasure, like groundlings at the theatre. When, earlier in the scene, Hal goaded him about his coward's 'instinct', nobody laughed at all. They seemed instead to hold their breath. But away from Falstaff's own presence, Hal's comic impersonation of Falstaff's run (a wide-legged, bear-like, side-to-side shamble) drew extravagant laughter. It was safe to laugh at him, when he was not there.

Indeed, in Part 2, it was altogether safer. Among the non-antagonistic company of the Gloucestershire yokels, Falstaff relaxed. He became positively torpid, arriving at Shallow's house asleep in the back of a wagon; after dinner, he was asleep again, nodding off on his bench in v i, oblivious now to Shallow, his beeves, and his country business-affairs. Even in the Part 2 tavern scene [II iv] there had been a tiredness about Falstaff's excuses concerning abusing the heir-apparent. The later brush with Prince John [IV iii] had also contained a significant detail: the subsequent speech in praise of sack was done with great gusto, except that, where Falstaff spoke of having a thousand sons, and addicting them all to sack, his voice dropped and wavered. We were reminded that he actually had no sons, except for the king's son who adopts him as a second father.

This small detail was consistent with a detectable new stress in Ackland's characterisation in Part 2. Falstaff's sense that there were things in life which were beyond his grasp could still provoke anger. Feeble's high-minded patriotism, in the Gloucestershire recruiting scenes, made Falstaff glower. Yet, just occasionally, the same sense of the unattainable went side by side with humane sympathy for others. The handling of the capture of Coleville [IV iii] in this production is of significance in this regard, and will be discussed elsewhere.

10 HAL AND OTHERS: 'I KNOW YOU ALL'

'Thus we play the fools with the time' – *Stratford 1964*

The interpretation of the play which has been most committed to the idea of a 'cold-blooded' Hal was the RSC 1964 version. Hal was played by Ian Holm, a physically ideal choice. Small, tidy, economical in his acting, everything about him contrasted with Hugh Griffith's Falstaff. Our first view of the two men was of them emerging from sleep from under the straw in a wagon. They went across to a pump, to douse each other with water. Falstaff was in a nightshirt the size of a bell-tent. Hal wore a neat dark doublet and hose. His physical appearance suggested Hamlet rather than a prodigal son.

Holm played the part neither primly nor censoriously. There were moments when his Hal seemed entirely at ease in the world of Eastcheap: the moments when he would lay an arm on Falstaff's shoulder, or allow himself to be picked up and hugged by the fat knight. Yet the impression was always of self-containment. In the great tavern scene of Part 1 [II iv], there was a good deal of laughter, but the joke was clearly on Falstaff rather than shared with him. One remembers Hal's turning his back on Falstaff's gouty tirade on cowardice, to shake with silent giggles; his assuming an expression of mock wonderment at Falstaff's Gadshill exploits; his bending over the fat knight in the chair, eye-brows raised, gleefully open-mouthed, his head giving little sharp nods, as he issued his challenge for Falstaff to wriggle out of the truth. It was all good fun, but the overwhelming impression of Hal's brand of humour was its stress on the ironic and the preposterous in what he saw around him. When Falstaff claimed, 'I knew ye', Hal turned away in disgust. When he 'deposed' Falstaff in the role of King Henry, in the 'mock reprimand', his expression became much tighter, and with Falstaff groping for comfort – 'banish not him thy Harry's company' – looked at him pitilessly as he said, 'I do, I will'. (For this episode, see Plate 1.)

Earlier, when Falstaff went to the door to investigate what the nobleman there wanted, Hal, in his absence, had already shown more than a hint of steely authority. As Falstaff disappeared up the stairs, Hal gave a little laugh, and then stopped. He looked at the others. They gave a little laugh, and stopped. Hal laughed again. They laughed again. Then, they clustered round him, to curry favour by excusing their own part in the cowardice and by ratting on Falstaff. Hal heard them with a mocking insolent smile.

Every other detail of Ian Holm's performance reinforced the impression of self-containment and control. His final interview with his father [2, IV iv] disclosed that he was capable of tears; but he gripped his father's hand tightly, at the bedside, choking them back. Always secretive, he rose at the end of this scene when he heard the others returning, so that nobody should see him in his father's arms. Earlier, when he took away the crown and placed it on his head, he moved slowly, staring into space like a sleep-walker. His face was absolutely neutral. When he actually ascended the throne legitimately [v ii], his quiet icy authority had finally found the role for which it was suited. His brothers, as one man, sank to their knees. As he walked through them, and away towards the exit, he made no attempt to encourage them to rise. As for Eastcheap, he had, until then, at best condescended to tolerate the company of his inferiors. On his coronation, he rejected Falstaff with exactly the same pitiless sadness anticipated so long before in the 'mock-reprimand' scene, as he looked down on the portly kneeling figure.

In the 1966 revival of this production (in fact, Ian Holm was one of only a very few survivors), the character of Hal had been pushed further down the same road. He seemed actively to enjoy giving pain. Yet the pain of others gave him no pleasure, no zest. Even in 1964, however, he had emerged as a joyless figure.

The point was made all the clearer by the carefully contrasted figure of Hotspur, lovingly portrayed by Roy Dotrice. This was a kilted, wild Hotspur, yet everything about him was full of warmth and exuberance. (See Plate 2.)

The major scene with his wife Lady Percy is often played as knockabout [1, ɪɪ iii]. In the Roy Dotrice/Janet Suzman version, it was still rough, but also very intimate, with a good deal of the scene played on the floor – husband and wife pushing over, kissing, tumbling, wrapping-up, kneeling astride or lying on top. Although Roy Dotrice is not physically large, everything about him seemed impressive. His accent was notably thicker than that of his kinsmen. Where every other warrior was content with a normal sword, Hotspur's was a huge two-handed cleaver.

In war, he was in his element. In anticipation of it, he had 'ridden' his saddle which his servant brought in on a saddle-stand. When the event arrived, he seemed on fire. All his restless energy, so evident from the very beginning, found its fulfilment as he leaped to do battle with Hal, laughing aloud as he swung the huge sword clanging against Hal's crossed sword and dagger, or forcing him to draw in his stomach like a hoop to escape it. Battles were an RSC speciality at this period. There were always hordes of extras, gun-smoke, cannon-fire and well-choreographed skirmishing. This fight, though, was exceptional. The audience feared for the physical safety of the two actors. And when finally, as they fought around a long horse-trough, and Hotspur's great sword thudded into the side of it, allowing Hal to get in and stab him under the ribs and lower him, dying, into the trough, there was what can only be described as a collective sigh from the audience. He had won the audience's love by his joy in life. Now he was dead; and curiously, the man who remained alive seemed to have no zest for life at all.

'A most princely hypocrite' – Television 1979

Not too far away from Ian Holm's interpretation was the 1979 television version, with David Gwillim as Hal. It was a more ambiguous performance than Holm's. David Gwillim seemed to have been cast as a fun-loving prince. His dimpled face seemed made for this kind of interpretation. In fact, it never really materialised. His laughter tended to have a scoffing quality. The scene with Poins in Part 2 [II ii], set in a grimy little wood-panelled room of an inn, was distinctly an edgy one, with Hal's confession of his distaste for his companions done as a calculated insult.

Above all, though, his relationship with Falstaff revealed a similar vein of detachment and distaste. In the great tavern scene of Part 1 [II iv], Hal was the one man among Falstaff's audience who was not won over by his performance. As Quayle's Falstaff prepared for the play of reprimand, Hal goaded him on the subject of his cowardly 'instinct'. His comments raised a laugh, trading as they did on Falstaff's own jokes and phrases, but Hal himself did not smile. When, during the reprimand-play, the roles were reversed, Hal as King Henry described Falstaff in a list of insults which were also delivered straight faced. The company began by laughing at these, willingly enough, still buoyed up by Falstaff's own performance as King Henry. Gradually, however, the laughter petered out. The scene became very still, and the only sound was of Hal's voice. The camera, moving in $\frac{1}{2}$-shot between the two men, registered the intentness in Hal, and the injured feelings in Falstaff. For Falstaff to keep up the pretence of good humour ('I would your grace would take me with you. Whom means your grace?') required a distinct effort. In his speech of self-defence, his habitual anxiety assumed the proportion of near-desperation. With the bustle of Bardolph noisily running in, and drawing everyone's attention, Hal's words 'I do, I will' were spoken quietly and meaningfully, and heard by Falstaff alone. He opened his mouth to speak, but no words came, as Hal still stared him down.

We have already seen how, in the television version, the relationship of Hal with his father, even in the final reconciliation, seemed depleted and distorted. Again, the production offered – as had the 1964 RSC version – the kind of Hotspur to make the point even clearer by contrast. As with the 1964 version, this Hotspur (in Tim Piggott-Smith's interpretation) was full of affection as well as vitality. With his fellow-conspirators he seemed perhaps no more than the mad-cap young lord, set off against the splendid laconic playing of his uncle Worcester by Clive Swift. With his wife Lady Percy, however, there was a great deal of coarse tenderness. In their major scene together [1, II iii], Piggott-Smith and Michele Dotrice played it with a smile, with lightness and humour. Hotspur's talk of love was scornful, yet done as boisterous teasing. His wife, not knowing whether to believe him, beat his chest with her tiny fists in frustration. The same tone was sustained in their farewell scene [1, III ii], where their physical contact was a constant rhythm of playful repulses and tender capture. Theirs seemed to have been a long and intimate friendship. When he tried to make her sing, like the Welsh lady, she betrayed in the surprising violence of her reply ('I will NOT sing') all the pent-up force of her anxiety at his departure.

The most memorable scene in either part of the play in this production was Lady Percy's lament for the death of her husband [2, II iii]. Elizabeth Moss's make-up scheme had achieved the difficult feat of making Michele Dotrice look dreadful. She walked a little aside from her parents-in-law for the speech, and the camera tightened in to close-up on her. It held that shot throughout the whole of her lament, except for one brief reaction-shot of a horror-struck Northumberland. She was barely able to begin speaking, managing to do so only by talking with deliberate slowness, one phrase at a time, pulling down her head, fighting off the tears. As the speech proceeded, her agonised face and voice went to the very edge of control. In her anguish, we had the final testimony to the kind of love Hotspur could inspire.

David Gwillim's Hal was a much better-looking man than
Hotspur, yet the face which contained the boyish smile and the
athletically-working mouth remained totally opaque. There
was nothing behind it. When he assumed the role of kingship,
he did so with a likable modesty. His rejection of Falstaff was
with a look of affecting pity. And yet, here as elsewhere, the
skin-deep attractiveness was designed to convey a man almost
without strong identity, whose every impulse was pallid. At the
very end, his voice subtly changed and took on something of the
stilted rhetorical air of his father's, again enhancing the sense
that there was almost no such person, no such identity as 'Hal'.
It was a very deeply studied playing, by David Gwillim, of a
very shallow man.

'Riot and dishonour stain the brow of my young Harry' – Stratford 1975

Perhaps the great divide, amongst the different types of Hal
available, is between those who drink and those who do not. In
neither the 1964 nor the television production can it be recalled
that Hal actually drank any wine. Perhaps another test is how
the director responds to a line of Falstaff's, spoken to Doll with
Hal present, in the tavern scene of Part 2: 'His grace [the
prince] says that which his flesh rebels against.' Some productions suggest at this point that Hal is experiencing the stirrings
of desire for Doll. Again, the 1964 and television Hals are not
guilty.

In both the 1975 and 1982 productions, however, Hal both
drank and felt desire. These very minor distinctions indicate a
quite different emphasis. In neither of these cases do we have a
'cold' Hal, but rather a creature of strong impulse.

As to the 1975 RSC version, Hal's relationship with his father
and with Falstaff – the triangular relationship which links them
– has already been explained. The other, earlier Hals had been
– however shallow – fully formed. This Hal of Alan Howard
was younger, and in the process of growing up. His speech, 'I
know you all' was delivered as a vague good intention, not as a
meticulous life-plan. His first real rebuff of Falstaff – 'I do, I
will' [1, II iv] – was produced when he had been badly stung by
a comment of Falstaff's own. The latter's line, on the subject of

Hal's enemies, 'Art thou not horribly afeared?' had produced a long and awkward silence. Falstaff had evidently struck a nerve, and had to suffer the consequences: discovering, in Hal's sharp promise of banishment, that playing with even the cub of a lion was not without its risks. Yet, the moment was a local collision, not a master-plan. It became increasingly clear that Hal was actually growing away from Falstaff, but the impulse never hardened into a scheme for his rejection. When, before the battle of Shrewsbury, Falstaff, sitting in a cart, tried to detain a now-brisk Hal from rushing away to battle by wrapping his legs around him, Hal wrenched free. Yet the prince seemed to be at pains almost to apologise for his escape, and did so in terms of the horse-play which typified their relationship, lobbing him an apple in a wave of farewell.

At the end of the plays, the emotional climax of the reconciliation with his father marked Hal's final growing-up. It was therefore a new man who, as Henry v, banished his old companion. The banishment began with a tremendously effective theatrical stroke. Farrah's set for the production had been until now very stark and bare. But, before the coronation-procession entered, stage-hands ran down from the back to the front of the stage, drawing down a huge white cloth over the stage behind them. Gold rushes were strewn on the white cloth. The lighting was suddenly brilliant. The bell that had tolled for the death of Henry iv now gave way to trumpets at the coronation of his son. The group of Falstaff's friends formed a ragged line from back to front down the stage-left depth of the stage. The new king's close family and allies entered, forming a similar line, stage-right. The contrast between the resulting two parallel lines was very strong. On the one side, there were the quaint cut-off smocks and wrinkled leggings of the rustics, the thonged-leather ballad-singer-like costume of Pistol, the curious Sinbad-like clothes of Bardolph. On the other were the pure white cloaks and scarlet St George's crosses of the crowned nobility, and the scarlet robe and golden chain of the Lord Chief Justice. The contrast was very considerably to the disadvantage of the first group. They looked a ragged mob. When therefore the king, in his coronation march, walked down the centre of the alleyway formed by the two lines, clad completely in golden armour from head to toe, a double-winged gold cape behind him, only to be halted by the kneeling figure of Falstaff in his carpet-bag-design coat, red hose and baggy boots, there could be no possible surprise at the rejection. (For this scene, see Plate 3.)

Henry V's was not only a new régime. It was to be a brilliant one. The dazzling splendour of the court party confirmed that. While we felt for Falstaff's pathetic blindness, there could be no doubt which choice Henry V must now make.

'Presume not that I am the thing I was' – Barbican 1982

By far the subtlest treatment of the role of Hal, however, was in the 1982 RSC production. If the actual standard of acting seemed at first unpromising in general in this production (compared, say, with the exceptionally gifted cast of 1964), there were marvellous compensations in the thoughtfulness of the interpretation.

As already mentioned, Gerard Murphy's Hal was a creature of impulse rather than of calculation. His version of 'I know you all' seemed surprisingly bitter. He appeared to snarl out the words, as he sat hunched on a barrel, loutishly picking his feet. The tone of the speech seemed to be, 'I'll show you', as if what he had in mind was scoring a point against his enemies. In the 'mock-reprimand', his dissatisfaction with a life of waste and pointlessness was evident. What began as a convincing impersonation of his father's stiff manner, complete with sips of cordial, became personally vituperative and savage as he spoke of Falstaff's vices.

In this production, however, Joss Ackland's Falstaff remained uncrushed. His, 'I would your grace would take me with you. Whom means your grace?' got a laugh that deflated Hal's urgency and irritated him still more. Falstaff's subsequent defence of tavern life was done with confidence, winning growls of approval from the stage-audience of drinkers. This too added to Hal's ill-temper, and when the promised rejection was spoken, it was thrown at Falstaff in the tone of a childish 'Yah', and with a nasty coarse laugh. As often happened in the inn-scenes of Trevor Nunn's production, nobody laughed with Hal.

Yet the same man was capable of great spontaneous affection for his fat friend. Immediately after the promise of rejection he gave Falstaff an ardent hug around the neck. When in Part 1 [IV ii], Falstaff with his cannon-fodder recruits met Hal on the road – or when, rather, Hal almost fell over him, since Falstaff was stretched out for a nap – the director altered the text so that Westmoreland's entry was not with Hal but delayed. By the time he did arrive, Hal and Falstaff were not only enjoying a good laugh together, but actually rolling on the floor, in tavern rough-and-tumble. They both scrambled guiltily to their feet when he entered. At the end of the great Tavern scene in Part 2 [II iv], Hal concluded his remarkably mild protests to Falstaff about being abusive to Doll and Quickly by gently kissing the old man on the cheek. It was a kind of fond farewell.

Again, the figure of Hotspur helped to form our response to Hal. Here, most unusually, he emerged (in Timothy Dalton's interpretation) not as a contrast but as a parallel. The warm-hearted side of him was played down, and replaced by moodiness. Many of his more 'poetic' lines were cut. His impulsiveness was much like Hal's own. In the first scene with his wife [1, II iii], he knelt, reading, as his wife came creeping downstairs. Played by Harriet Walter as a very submissive lady, she crouched beside him. The two figures became, suddenly, two people talking about their marriage. They looked grim and lugubrious. Hotspur jumped up, to call for his horse. Lady Percy followed, attempting playfully to wheedle his secrets out of him. Quite suddenly he turned on her. The line, 'Away, you trifler' was delivered with ferocious force. When he said, 'I care not for thee, Kate', there was no doubt that he meant it. If at the end he relented, holding out a hand to her which eventually she took, the patching-up of their marriage was only temporary. In their only other scene together [1, III ii] – a scene which is usually nothing more than a piece of pleasant domestic nonsense, with the Welsh lady's song – Hotspur's declared fancy for the Welsh lady's bed looked all too probably true. When his wife took offence and refused to sing as requested, he seemed deliberately to pick a quarrel on this trivial matter in order to break away and leave her.

Earlier in that scene, listening to Worcester's lecture on good manners, Hotspur again produced an unexpected and unusual emphasis on 'Well, I am *schooled*', sarcastically slapping his own wrist. Throughout this scene he had sulked at Glendower, the silken Celtic diplomat. Again, he was trying to pick a fight. Like Hal, he was a difficult man. Trevor Nunn's direction gave particular emphasis to their various envious speeches about each other. They were alike; and this made much more sense than usual of their rivalry.

Yet the most intriguing point of all in this production was that Hotspur was not really Hal's worst enemy.

If Hal emerged, in Gerard Murphy's interpretation, as a deeply unhappy man, it was not merely because he was unhappy and unsettled with tavern life. Far more disturbing to him was the divided response he felt towards his own family. This division of feeling was something particularly concentrated on a pair of figures who emerged almost as the villains of the production: Hal's brother, Prince John, and his nearest friend and ally, Westmoreland (played, respectively, by Kevin Wallace and Bernard Brown).

The production gave full weight to the idea which Hal expressed during the battle of Shrewsbury: that his father's mind had been poisoned against him. In the very first scene, we saw Westmoreland at work, doing the poisoning. The king was speaking of the 'gallant' prowess of Hotspur. Westmoreland responded very pointedly: 'In faith, /   It is a conquest for a *prince* to boast of.' The loaded emphasis, and the significant look which accompanied it, transformed an innocent speech into a veiled insinuation, hinting at the deficiencies of the king's own son. When Hal finally appeared at court [1, III ii] and approached his father, the nobles who left the chamber brushed past him, looking him up and down and snubbing him. At the end of Part 1 Prince John evidently resented Hal's reconciliation with his father. When Hal offered his brother the 'gift' of the honour of releasing the Douglas without ransom, Kevin Wallace interpreted the lines, 'I thank your grace for this high courtesy, /   Which I shall give away immediately', as, 'thanks for nothing: I can't wait to get rid of *that* gift'.

By Part 2 it became clear that Hal's dislike of his younger brother was well-founded. It was Prince John, not Hal, who seemed to be faking grief on the death of their father. The Gaultree Forest scenes, difficult to condone at the best of times, were so directed as to give full weight to the unpleasantest side of Prince John and Westmoreland. Both became sour-faced sermonisers in their speeches to the rebels, so that their show of piety made their own deviousness all the more repellent. It clearly came hard to Westmoreland to have to kiss the archbishop's hand. Prince John made a much better job of it, emerging as a super-smooth hypocrite, with a glittering smile, which slipped when he was not seen, but was carefully replaced whenever a rebel turned to him. It was clearly, for John, a moment of revenge for having earlier been forced to kiss the archbishop's hand, when he seized it to arrest him, made a mock-gesture of raising it to his lips, but then tore from the hand its ring of office.

The equation was made very clear: of the zeal and clean-living of Hal's young brother, and the operation of politics at its most cynical and inhumane. Slightly against the text, the archbishop's faction came over by contrast as well-meaning innocents.

Even Falstaff was used to reinforce this impression. In Joss Ackland's interpretation, there was no great stress on Falstaff as predator. Rather, he turned out finally to seem to vindicate the claims he had made in Part 1, that his real affinity was with whatever was humane. On the one occasion when Prince John met Falstaff [2, IV iii], the latter had just captured a prisoner, one Coleville. He was much inclined to gloat over the fact, oblivious to the agonies of embarrassment this inflicted on Coleville. Yet when Prince John smirkingly sentenced Coleville to death, Falstaff registered horror. There was an interesting repeat of these two contrasted reactions at the very end of Part 2, with Prince John enthralled at the prospect of Hal's launching a foreign war, but the Lord Chief Justice clearly deeply disturbed at the thought. The inhumanity of the pious and of their agents was again shown in the brief scene [2, v iv] featuring the purge of the brothels and the arrest of Doll, in which her captors tried to rape her.

With brutality and ruthlessness so clearly personified in John and Westmoreland, Hal's truancy in Eastcheap finally fell very clearly into place. It was a matter of his instinctive recoil from the tainted politics of his father's reign. Turning from the 'respectable' world, he made his gesture of rejection as pointed as possible by keeping the vilest company he could find. Of course, he could never be at ease in Eastcheap. He too clearly despised his own waste and riot, and was all too inclined to take it out on his companions. A neat detail here was the way in which the boy-waiter Francis, about to curl up asleep on the floor at the end of Part 2, II iv, warily circled around Hal, keeping well out of reach. At this stage, Hal's only profit from Eastcheap was to pick up the trick of fighting dirty (Bardolph in battle was an expert groin-kicker!) which he put to good use in killing Hotspur with a knife under the ribs and across the throat.

Yet Eastcheap was Hal's only outlet for his undoubted capacity to love and to give affection. In Part 2, with the sub-plot so clearly identified with harmlessness, fun and humanity – at least, as much of them as was possible in the edgy and destructive régime of a usurper – Hal's choice of low-life made complete human sense. When, prematurely taking the crown, he placed it on his own head, he did so with no appearance of pleasure or awe. Rather, with a clumsy ugly gesture, he jammed it on his thatch of hair. Its advent brought only grief: partly for the death of his father, but more for the loss of his own treasured escape-route from the contamination of politics. At his coronation procession, in his new public role, he seemed like a man in a daze. When he rejected Falstaff, he deliberately stepped outside the line of the coronation procession, and for those few lines, regained expressiveness, delivering his verdict with a strained smile, choking off a sob. When he resumed his place in the procession, his face was again a blank. The moment symbolised the loss of humanity which his new role entailed, and the extent that humanity had been represented by his old companion. (See Plate 6.)

Intriguingly, at the end of the procession walked the figure of Poins. Against the indications in the text, it seemed that Poins had survived where Falstaff had not. Beautifully played as a cool cynic by Miles Anderson, he had throughout enjoyed a slightly different kind of intimacy with Hal from the others in the tavern: the relationship perhaps of two ex-public-schoolboys. Incapable of being provoked, and with the happy knack of not provoking Hal overmuch, Poins had made himself indispensable. The new king desperately needed human contact, consigned as he now was to the loveless world of the court. Poins, respectable enough to be salvaged from Eastcheap, was the one friend Hal had left.

11 CONCLUSIONS

The performing theatre arts have an extraordinarily broad license in interpreting the plays they perform. In effect, the very marked differences of emphasis from production to production represent the working evidence of widely disparate critical interpretations. Opinions will always continue to shift, and new productions will continue to disclose new resources in the plays.

The key figure is inevitably Hal. Whatever a production does with other key figures matters less than what it does with Hal. Versions of Falstaff might differ widely, as these four have; but his status in the play will always be basically the same, as the chosen focus of Hal's truancy. A new interpretation of King Henry as, say, an abrasive self-made man (as in the 1975 RSC production) may be inventive and pleasing. Yet still, his basic function in the play will likewise be the same: as suffering usurper, and inadequate father.

Yet the chosen nature of Hal in any given production will necessarily condition and entail so much else. If Hal is shallow (as in the TV production) or cold and withdrawn (as in 1964), the corollary is automatically that Hotspur or Falstaff or the Gloucestershire scenes will and must emerge as 'warm'. If Hal is, on the other hand, played as impulsive or immature (as in 1982 and 1975), then the Hotspur contrast tends to be obliterated entirely. Far more significantly, so does the contrast with Eastcheap.

Both approaches have support in the text, and the 1964 and 1982 versions particularly vividly represent the possibilities of each. Notably, in both versions, Hal is trapped between court and tavern; though in one case nothing at all touches the Prince, while in the other he is racked with conflicting emotions towards both worlds. The second interpretation is more humanly comprehensible. The first makes more sense of the idea of a man awaiting a national destiny, which the plays undoubtedly contain. Inevitably, the most recent of the productions we have discussed tends to seem the most persuasive. Fortunately the play is big enough to accommodate both interpretations.

READING LIST

J. Russell Brown, *Discovering Shakespeare: A New Guide to the Plays* (Macmillan: London and Basingstoke, 1981). This advises the student of the text of a play on its 'theatricality' and on the various ways of translating written words into stage action and role-performance. For *Henry IV*, see especially pp. 145–56.

Lily B. Campbell, *Shakespeare's 'Histories': Mirrors of Elizabethan Policy* (Huntington Library, San Marino, Cal., 1947). Though its interpretation has in some respects been subjected to criticism in recent years, this is still immensely useful in giving political and historiographical background to the History plays.

S. C. Sen Gupta, *Shakespeare's Historical Plays* (Oxford UP, 1964).

G. K. Hunter (ed.), *Shakespeare: Henry IV, Parts 1 and 2* (Macmillan Casebook series, London and Basingstoke, 1970). A selection of critical studies.

Emrys Jones, *Scenic Form in Shakespeare* (Oxford UP, 1971).

J. McLaverty, 'No Abuse: The Prince and Falstaff in the Tavern Scenes of *Henry IV*', in *Shakespeare Survey*, 34, ed. K. Muir (Cambridge UP, 1981), pp. 105–10.

A. C. Sprague, *Shakespeare's Histories: Plays for the Stage* (Society for Theatre Research, London, 1964). This study approaches the plays through production possibilities and theatre history.

E. M. W. Tillyard, *Shakespeare's History Plays* (Chatto and Windus, London, 1944; reprinted 1974). A classic study, though challenged in recent years by other interpretations.

John Wilders, *The Lost Garden: A View of Shakespeare's English and Roman History Plays* (Macmillan: London and Basingstoke, 1978; reprinted 1982). This identifies certain prominent ideas which appear in all the History plays, and strongly challenges the Tillyard interpretation. For *Henry IV*, see especially pp. 23–5, 50–2, 86–91, 110–11.

J. Dover Wilson, *The Fortunes of Falstaff* (Cambridge UP, 1943). This contains a cogent theory of Falstaff as tempter.

James Winny, *The Player King* (Chatto and Windus, London, 1968).

WIDENER UNIVERSITY
WOLFGRAM
LIBRARY
CHESTER, PA.

INDEX